LONDON
STRATEGIC

POLICY UNIT

RACISM AWARENESS

TRAINING

– A CRITIQUE

LONDON AGAINST RACISM

ISBN: 1 8700 130 3 4

TYPESETTING, COVER DESIGN, LAYOUT AND PRINTING BY
HANSIB PUBLISHING LTD,
TOWER HOUSE,
139/149 FONTHILL ROAD,
LONDON N4 3HF ENGLAND.
TEL 01 281 1191 TELEX 22294

RACE EQUALITY POLICY GROUP: KEY CONTACTS

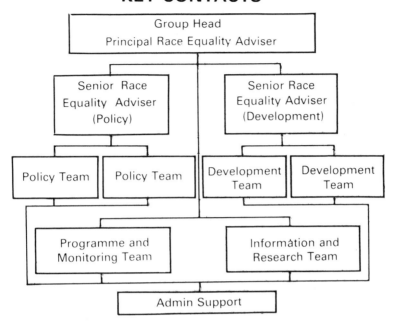

PRINCIPAL RACE EQUALITY ADVISER
Ansel Wong   633 4537

SENIOR RACE EQUALITY ADVISER (DEVELOPMENT)
Pat Lee-Sang   633 2159

SENIOR RACE EQUALITY ADVISER (POLICY)
Richard Seager   633 3701

TEAM LEADERS (POLICY)
Rekha Prashar   633 3701
Akyaaba Addai-Sebo   633 3655

TEAM LEADERS (DEVELOPMENT)
Vacancy   633 3701
Amin Cajee   633 3675

PROGRAMME AND MONITORING TEAM
Charlotte Slade   633 3607

INFORMATION AND RESEARCH TEAM
Vacancy   633 3603

Acknowledgements

REPG would like to thank A. Sivanandan and Race
and Class and Ahmed Gurnah and Sheffield
Polytechnic for permission to reprint their articles.

RAT and the degradation of the black struggle
first appeared in
Race and Class, XXVI, 4 (1985), pp1-33

The Politics of Racism Awareness Training
first appeared in
Critical Social Policy, Issue No. 11,
Winter 1984, pp6-20.

CONTENTS

Appendix A

Appendix B

Introduction

A significant outcome of the 1981 uprisings was the impetus which they gave to Racism Awareness Training (RAT). While a number of organisations which practised RAT existed from 1978 onwards, these organisations gained little public recognition up until 1981. Yet, following the urban uprisings and the Scarman inquiry, RAT quickly came to be seen as a panacea in the struggle against racism. Most of the local authorities and other public sector bodies which expanded their race equality work in the wake of the uprisings devoted a considerable amount of resources to RAT. Taking on board some of the recommendations made by Scarman, a number of local authorities began to send their staff on RAT courses. It was argued that institutional racism was a corollary of 'ignorance' and a lack of awareness about the problems facing ethnic minorities. Hence, an effective assault on institutional racism could be mounted by making the workforce of public bodies aware of racial issues and challenging the prejudices of individual employees. Thus, RAT, which can be defined as training designed to challenge racism in individuals and institutions, became fashionable, and the tiny handful of RAT organisations which existed prior to 1981 experienced a mercurial growth. RAT courses soon became a standard feature in the police force, schools, colleges and local authorities, and, in order to meet the growing demand for RAT trainers, a gamut of new RAT organisations were established.

Right from the inception of RAT in Britain, a number of community activists and academic writers were highly critical of the practice and questioned its utility in the struggle against racism. Moreover, they argued, RAT was being used to deflect attention away from genuine anti-racist struggles, and, as such, was an obstacle in the battle to eradicate racism from British institutions. These views were expressed most forcefully by Ahmed Gurnah [1] and A. Sivanandan [2] In response to this growing controversy about RAT and the fact that the Greater London Council (GLC) provided assistance for organisations to avail themselves of RAT, the Ethnic Minorities Unit of the GLC decided to hold a conference on the subject as part of its consultation programme and in an effort to review the Council's own policy in relation to anti-racist training.

The Conference

The conference, entitled 'Racism Awareness Training – A Critique', was held on Sunday 28 July 1985 at County Hall. It had four main objectives:

1. To provide a forum in which to debate the current controversy about RAT.

2. To examine the effectiveness of RAT courses.

3. To provide an opportunity for the black and other ethnic minority communities to put forward their views on RAT.

4. To solicit proposals and recommendations which could assist the GLC in formulating its policy on RAT.

The conference was attended by over 400 delegates, with many more expressing a keen interest. Having been prominently advertised in the black press and a number of national newspapers and magazines, the conference received participants from many authorities outside of London, such as Sheffield, Leicester, Coventry, Colchester, Reading, Manchester and Milton Keynes. The backgrounds of the delegates were extremely varied, and among those present were social workers, teachers, lecturers, community activists, race advisers, youth workers, anti-racism campaigners and RAT trainers.

The morning session was devoted to a panel discussion comprising six speakers:

Ahmed Gurnah (Lecturer, Sheffield City Polytechnic).

Pamela Nanda (former Race Relations Adviser, Ethnic Minorities Unit).

Sybil Phoenix (Director, Methodist Leadership Racism Awareness Workshop)

Colin Prescod (Lecturer, Polytechnic of North London and Institute of Race Relations).

Gus John (Senior Officer, Manchester Education Department).

Sabina Sharkey (Irish anti-racism campaigner).

The afternoon session was devoted to workshop discussions with a plenary session at the end. During this final session, the following proposals were submitted for future consideration and implementation by the GLC. However, limited follow-up work was undertaken on these recommendations because of the abolition of the Council. The main recommendations were:

(a)   The GLC should stop funding RAT courses.

(b)   The money that is being spent on RAT should be given to black and other ethnic minority organisations.

(c)   A distinction should be made between anti-racist training and RAT.

(d)   Training should concentrate on institutional racism and equip people to eradicate discriminatory practices in their place of work.

(e)   The GLC should set up a forum to counter imperialism and racism in London.

(f)   The GLC should examine its employment policy towards the Irish, who are an ethnic minority but are not monitored by the Equal Opportunities programme.

(g)   There needs to be agreement on what anti-racist training should consist of, and everybody employed as a trainer in this field should undergo an agreed form of training.

(h)   More visual aid material should be produced for anti-racism training

(i)   Anti-racist education should be a part of the mainstream school curriculum and not marginalised as at present.

(j)   Anti-racist training should be an integral part of teacher training.

(k)   Race advisers should become actively involved in black struggle and look upon the black community as their power base.

(l)   Race advisers should not accept white definitions of black political struggle, but develop their own concepts in collaboration with the black community.

(m)   Anti-racist training should only take place in the context of, and as an integral part of, a specific anti-racist programme of work designed to uncover racial discrimination within organisations and bring about racial equality.

These recommendations continue to remain pertinent to local government despite the absence of a strategic authority for London. Fortunately, the effects of such an absence have been muted somewhat by the presence of the London Strategic Policy Unit (LSPU).

Post GLC Abolition

With the abolition of the GLC, it was feared that many of the programmes
and initiatives – particularly the very innovative and pioneering policies on
equalities – would be killed off. Thus in an effort to maintain and continue
these programmes, nine London Councils – Lambeth, Hackney, Haringey,
Lewisham, Greenwich, Islington, Ealing, Camden and Southwark – formed
the London Strategic Policy Unit (LSPU) in March 1986 to carry forward
some of the GLC's most significant work. The LSPU was set up under the
provisions of the Local Government Act 1972 to carry out research and
information work on seven key policy areas – recreation and the arts, race
equality, economic policy, planning policy, transport, police monitoring and
research, and women's equality.

In order to provide a comprehensive strategy for the needs and concerns
of all Londoners, an integrated approach for the seven policy areas was
devised. This approach therefore centred around four primary themes: the
fight against poverty, the preservation and expansion of democracy, the
struggle for equality and the improvement of London's environment.

A Strategic Policy On Race Equality

Despite the initiative taken by the GLC and a number of local authorities,
racism remains a major obstacle affecting the life chances of Britain's black
and other ethnic minority communities. Racism is endemic in our society and
therefore affects us all, especially in the areas of employment and the
provision of services. The first challenge is to accept this basic fact and from
this acknowledgment should flow initiatives to challenge and eventually
eradicate racism.

The LSPU believes that this can be done through the adoption of a race
equality policy and the development of a range of advisory and supportive
services which must form part of a co-ordinated strategy to eliminate
structural, institutional, and individual racism. But policies by themselves are
inadequate without a political context. LSPU will give highest priority to
understanding and analysing this political context which sustains the
existence of racism. The ultimate goal of this two-pronged process – policies
and politics – will be to develop a coherent alternative strategy which will
ensure uninhibited access for black and other ethnic minority communities to
power, resources, and services.

LSPU further believes that the challenge to racism must also incorporate
the promotion of equal opportunity employer policies, the active participation
of the black and other ethnic minority communities themselves, the struggles

against sexism, homophobia, and all forms of discrimination, the development of a high level of public awareness of the issues, and the allocation of sufficient resources to make them a reality. The Race Equality Policy Group (REPG) was thus set up, within LSPU, to do precisely that.

The Race Equality Policy Group (REPG)

The REPG gives priority consideration to the development of a political awareness of how race, together with other variables of class and gender, underpin the community struggles for justice and freedom. Through specialist knowledge and the collation and analysis of data, the REPG is able to provide individual boroughs with the information necessary to initiate and monitor change at all levels.

Having the opportunity to develop a strategic and coordinated overview of many of the central concerns in combating racism, either through evaluation of present practices and past experiences or innovative research programmes, REPG offers the boroughs a unique service which will ensure an integrated approach to equal opportunities, and to anti-racism in particular.

Part of this service is the development of a central resource specialising in research, analyses, and an ability to respond quickly to urgent issues and developments. For example, REPG compiles individual borough profiles according to ethnicity/race using both quantitative and qualitative research methods. From such profiles, each borough will be able to extract information according to demographic and service-based characteristics in defining its priorities and policies for dealing with discrimination and gaps in services.

REPG's programme includes work with the voluntary sector, travellers, the Irish community, migrants and refugees, anti-deportation campaigns, and deals with issues such as racism in the media, positive action programmes in training and employment, racism and mainstream institutions, anti-apartheid and local authorities, anti-racist education, young people, racial harassment and attacks, and racism and linguistic minorities. It also works on the specific needs of black and other ethnic minority communities in the health service, social services, education, environmental health, housing, transport and planning, and looks at issues which affect black workers in trade unions. To carry out these programmes, a number of teams have been formed.

Policy Teams

The Policy Teams work on policy areas; advising and working with boroughs on specific policy initiatives. This work is largely to ensure a race dimension and implementation of policies in local authorities. The team will ensure there is inter-borough collaboration, especially in areas of grant-aid, training, and the framework of consultation, bearing in mind existing services and provisions both in local authorities and other statutory organisations such as the Arts Council and the Greater London Arts Association.

Development Teams

There are two Development Teams whose primary responsibility is to develop, through liaison and outreach work, proposals on important issues which affect all ethnic minority communities. Such proposals, when linked up with work done in the policy teams, will be concentrated on specific communities – Asian, African, Caribbean, travellers, Irish, Cypriots, migrants and refugees – as well as on major concerns – immigration, nationality, translations and interpretations.

Programme monitoring team

This team assumes full responsibility for monitoring and evaluating the progress of the REPG's work programme and budget as well as undertaking all tasks associated with the Group's consultation programme and anti-racist initiatives.

Information and Research team

This team services all other teams in the REPG and is responsible for the collection and collation of all data on race. In fulfilling this function, it has the remit to establish a reference library, and data bank as well as the capacity to undertake or supervise major research projects which analyse issues from a 'race specific' perspective.

The publication of this report, therefore, goes towards fulfilling commitment to continue the initiatives begun by the GLC. Racism Awareness Training is still perceived as a panacea for local authority ills and the publication of this report is a timely reminder to officers and members of progressive local authorities of the need to re-evaluate RAT. We hope that the information and analysis contained in this report will fuel this reconsideration and help to put an end to RAT as it is presently perceived.

Ansel Wong
Principal Race Equality Adviser, LSPU.
December 1986

Footnotes

1. Ahmed Gurnah, The 'Politics of Racism Awareness Training', *Critical Social Policy*, Issue No. 11, Winter 1984, pp 6-20 (Appendix A).
2. A. Sivanandan, 'RAT and the degradation of black struggle', *Race and Class*, vol. 26 No. 4, 1985, pp 1-33 (Appendix B).

Introductory Remarks:
Fitzroy Ambursley,
Information and Research Officer, GLC

As many of you are aware racism awareness training has been one of the fastest growth areas in the British economy over the last few years. It has been quite booming in fact, and yet a number of black people, both trainers and those who have been trained, have expressed a number of reservations about the contents of this training, its utility in the struggle against racism, what the way forward is and whether, in fact, we should be getting involved in this. In response to the criticisms that have been expressed by the community, academics and individual members of the community, the Ethnic Minorities Unit has organised this conference. We see this conference as a form of consultation. This conference has been called to solicit ideas and recommendations from you, the community, so that the GLC can formulate its own policy on this matter.

I would like to make it clear that this is a completely open debate and open forum; we're not here to either support RAT or oppose it; we want to hear from you. We would welcome contributions both in favour of the training from people who have been involved with the training, as well as from people who have been critical of it. You may notice that most of the speakers on the platform will tend to be more critical of Racism Awareness Training, and the sole reason for this is that most of the people who are arch-proponents of RAT did not want to come to the conference to speak. When we invited them to come along and be keynote speakers, some of the leading advocates of Racism Awareness Training declined that offer, and so that is why the composition of the panel is as it is.

The first speaker, Ahmed Gurnah, from Sheffield City Polytechnic, has written an important article on the question of Racism Awareness Training.

Ahmed Gurnah
Sheffield City Polytechnic

I've come here not to support RAT but to oppose it. In 1981 the situation of black people in Britain looked pretty grim indeed, and people on the whole felt that it looked grim. In 1985, the situation has got worse, but for some reason it doesn't look like it's got worse, and some of the responsibility for that has to do with Racism Awareness Training. I'm not suggesting that RAT made the situation worse for black people in Britain, but I think the responsibility for not pointing out that things have been getting worse are to do with the kind of things that proponents of RAT have been doing. I'll try and substantiate my assertion.

One of the good things that Racism Awareness Training has done on the whole is it has helped to put the issue of racism on the agenda in some of the very obscure recesses of Town Halls and State Departments. Even before that, as most black people who've worked in these institutions will tell you, if you ever raised the issue of racism you were either told you had a chip on your shoulder, or that this was not relevant, or you were too preoccupied with it, or that they were all liberals and nobody actually thought of you as any different, and so on. One thing that Racism Awareness Training has done, over the last four years is make that kind of response more difficult. I'm not saying that it doesn't happen, but it's more difficult. That has to be a good thing, but having said that, everything else I have to say has to be negative. The main objection I have is that both the mode they have chosen for achieving the kind of things that they're after, and the assumptions that Racism Awareness trainers make are not sufficient to meet the kind of objectives they set for themselves.

The mode chosen tends to be psychologistic and individualistic. The assumption made is that if you enlighten individuals this will lead to correct political action, and that these individuals can now act correctly in the way that you would like them to act. This mode that has been chosen and this assumption that has been made are the root cause of the problem of Racism Awareness Training.

For example, as far as the assumption is concerned one of the things that is often banded about is this stock phrase: prejudice + power = racism. Behind that phrase, there is an assumption that the reason for racism is that there are some people who have power, and at the same time they are prejudiced. If you had that equation in front of you then you can see how easy it would be to deal with racism, because all you would have to do is topple prejudice then the power tumbles over and falls down over these very nice people who used to be racist before, and now that they are not prejudiced anymore they are prepared to give up their power. That is very unlikely and it's very naive in many ways and that is the root assumption of Racism Awareness Training.

I agree with the objectives that are set, and one of the objectives is that they want to deconstruct racist history. The other objective is that they want to advertise and counter racism in popular culture. In other words, racism that comes out of language relating to each other in the classroom, in public or in the office. They want to challenge the sub-structure of society and relations in society which allow exploitation of black people. I'm not convinced that people are equipped to deal with these objectives. It's not like someone taking a hammer to a knife, it is more like taking a stick of celery to a coconut. What they suggest is not effective enough to deal with the kind of problems that they set out or that they want to deal with.

My specific objection is that increasing understanding about racism in a liberal institution gets us nowhere because the issue is not about whether people have understood or not, it is about whether they are prepared to give up certain privileges that they have to someone else. I haven't seen any evidence of this. People have been trying to make the liberal establishment understand the oppression of the working class for years, but it doesn't seem to have made much difference. Capitalism in any case is not motivated by goodwill. You are not going to change structures whose foundation is capitalist oppression, and RAT has been involved in that process or is a consequence of that process. You're not going to change the system by just making a few officers in the Town Hall feel guilty.

Finally, and perhaps more directly important for strategies and political action, RAT has diverted a lot of previously very active political people from the kind of activities they used to be involved in, which was mainly to organise black people to organise amongst themselves, to raise issues within the community and against the State. All of those types of activities, all those types of more direct and relevant political activities, have been replaced by the activity of getting a few people in a room and making them feel guilty. That perhaps is the most frightening of the recent changes. People's energies are being misdirected, and quite a lot of people who used to be involved in politics directly in the way I have described it, have got involved in Racism Awareness Training instead, and that is very damaging. It shifts the struggle away from the real issues of organising in the community and organising against State control.

Pamela Nanda,
Former Race Relations Adviser, GLC

When I was asked to speak here about Racism Awareness Training I began to think quite carefully about my own involvement and the move from thinking some years ago that it was like the 'B's and 'E's to thinking that it's a total waste of time. This process that I and other people went through is important in illustrating, from my personal experiences, some aspects of the controversy over the relevance and importance of RAT.

I joined 'the race industry' in Bradford some years ago along with eight or ten other Section 11 black workers and we were split into different Directorates and different Departments and the majority of us knew little or nothing about local authorities. At that time, certainly in the north of England where race industries were being set up, it wasn't an uncommon scenario.

Because we were all separated into different areas with very little knowledge about local government and local authorities, we began to build a support group amongst ourselves. Bradford had concentrated its resources into training, and, perhaps unusually for a local authority, had always invested a lot of money and time into training staff. A lot of that training was related to some kind of human relations training.

Having built up this support group, the training area became a power base for people who were otherwise fairly isolated within the system. Within that power base and within training the one area that we were allowed to go into was race training, and it was called Racism Awareness Training. In that area we had time, money and resources, and an enormous amount of freedom; freedom that we weren't given in any other area of local authority work. The 'catch model', which a lot of Racism Awareness Trainers used, was largely rejected and people did come up with, in terms of innovative ideas, some good ideas about how to put over very difficult concepts. One of the areas, for example, was around deportation. In Bradford there were a number of deportation cases that were being fought but many of the workers never joined the fight. But throughout that time there were very, very few 'born again anti-racists'. Largely it produced tears, anger, guilt and a lot of money that was not spent on the black community. It did not increase the numbers of employees in the council significantly nor did it improve services to the black community. Instead they virtually invited black people to come in from the community and do Racism Awareness Training.

The other side of that was the result of what happened to many of the black Section 11 workers. Many were very, very angry and frustrated; they felt marginalised. Sometimes they were seen as militant and ultimately the worst thing that happened was that in-fighting began. The power base which people thought that they had was toppling over, but it hadn't been there in the first place. With in-fighting, frustration and anger many left. Some of them became race advisors to carry on in the race industry. I'm doing some research at the moment for the Local Government Training Board on the training needs of race advisors, and one of the interesting things that I've found is that the only race advisers who think that Racism Awareness Training is any good are those who ae actually new to the local authority for it brings back pictures of the past. In the GLC, Racism Awareness Training has made people into good racists, so that when you look at grievance procedures, people have used the right language, done all the right things, but they've become incredibly clever at blocking, and that blocking has been a learned process. They know the right things to do. The training that has gone on in this building deals with behaviour as opposed to attitudes. But I'm not sure even now that behavioural change is an easy thing to do or that training is necessarily the right way of doing it because at the end of the day black people are still fighting for the same things. Organisational change does require action and training might come up with some good ideas occasionally, but it is still dependent upon senior management and politicians and all sorts of other people.

Sybil Phoenix
Director, Methodist Leadership Racism Awareness Workshop

I need to be positive to begin with because I believe in what I am doing. I am not saying that what my other two colleagues have put forward hasn't got value, but I would like to defend what I believe in.

There is a saying that if somebody is hungry and they can't get bread and butter that you can at least give them biscuits. When I started working in this country some thirty years ago I faced racism, but it was the kind of racism that you couldn't come out and say "That is racism". It was there; it hit you very hard. I came here as a trained person but couldn't get a job because my training wasn't valid in England; it was done in South America. One started from there because one had to; one was thrown in at the deep end and one had to do something about it.

I was brought up in the Christian religion and I am aware of what the white churches have done to the Third World, to my parents and to me, but I am a firm believer in the man: Jesus Christ. That is my ideology. I believe that, and because I believe that I am sitting here defending it. I feel that the experience I have acquired over the years of trying to open the door so that other black people can walk through, I can use in the churches to try to do something about making space for black people. In 1972 I started this work in the churches and I am still trying to open those doors.

Everybody likes to sit on beautiful beaches, but have you ever looked at the grain of sand? Without the first grain of sand you couldn't have the beach. It is that grain of sand I am concerned with because if I can mould that grain, then the beach will be even more beautiful. There is a saying that if you throw mud, some will stick. I am not throwing mud, I am trying to be more dignified and so I am throwing cement, and I am throwing cement for two reasons. I feel that cement has more resilience than mud and the people on whom I have managed to get some cement to stick are the firm ones and they can help to carry the banner. I am throwing cement because there is a life in it. Racism has a destructive life of its own when it is not attended to. To do nothing is to give your vote to the status quo. I am not prepared to sit on the fence. If you don't use your voice then in the end you will have no voice; if you don't use your vote then you become useless because you haven't exercised your right. Brothers and sisters, I am exercising my right to continue to be the thorn in white society and the church. I have decided that I will be the thorn in their sides, and I will always be there to say "It isn't right. It shouldn't be", and as long as God gives me breath I shall continue to do that.

Colin Prescod
Lecturer, Polytechnic of North London and Institute of Race Relations

Having agreed to speak, I knew that there was no need for a lengthy speech from the platform, but in fact the most exciting part of what should happen is that you out there ought to be talking. You ought to be saying what we have to do. My suspicion is that you don't need to be made aware of racism, just as you don't need to be made aware of the critique of RAT, since Gurnah's essay, and Siva's excellent essay more importantly, (see Appendix B) have both been circulated for some months now and have been much discussed.

I am here to bury RAT because RAT has reached quite disturbing proportions. Gurnah has already talked about that in his own way. In a very specific sense for me, racist establishment institutions are today reaching for RAT exactly in order to avoid political anti-racist challenges. I know this about the very place that I work for , the Polytechnic of North London. We've had a fascist attending classes there for the last year and a half; a leading member of the National Front. We've had courageous students there, black and white, some of whom went to prison because they objected to having a fascist around who would name them and who was encouraging the attacks on black people in this society. We, students and lecturers, struggled to get the institution to take effective action and really implement its much trumpeted policy to give recognition to race, class and sex issues. Instead, we had protestations about democracy and free speech. We came out of that long struggle and my Polytechnic at this moment is proposing to have what it calls an anti-racist policy, but one which really is an equal opportunities policy. Just that – equal opportunities! Do we want equal opportunities to enter the police force? Do we want equal opportunities to become officers who stop black people coming into the country under the racist legislation? That is what they are proposing. They are allocating £15,000 for all members of my Polytechnic to have a Racism Awareness Training course. This is how they will prove that they are anti-racist while they are refusing to take on the political challenges of anti-racism. This is why I said earlier that Racism Awareness Training has reached quite staggering proportions and it's come right into my court, and that's why I came here to bury RAT, not simply to criticise it.

Having read the essays by Gurnah and Sivanandan (Appendix A and B), we understand how and why RAT has arisen. It arises in the moment of what Sivanandan has called in one of his lovely phrases, "The flight of race from class", which has occurred in black political struggle in this country recently. It is a large phrase. It means that we have moved more and more into the ghettoes of the safety of working amongst our own kind rather than thinking about how our struggles expand out to class struggle, community and class struggles making a larger political contribution. That has been a tendency.

It is also true that Racism Awareness Training has come into existence because there has been a shift, a slide from focusing on the institutionalised racism that we're struggling against to a focus on racial disadvantage. Note that if you focus only on racial disadvantage you are back into equal opportunities again. Remove the racial disadvantage so that we can enter into the existing institutions, and presto 'disadvantage' disappears. But that merely changes the racial composition of the workforce and leaves the institutions to continue to oppress and exploit. That is why we cannot simply be focusing on racial disadvantage.

We can understand how RAT came into existence because we have experienced a fragmentation of the black community in this society; some of us have participated in that but the State has encouraged and engendered it too. We understand all that, but simply to understand it is not to tolerate it.

Let me emphasise why we must reject and bury RAT. First of all, RAT is a con. It's a con in a variety of ways. It's in the first instance an intellectual social science con. It's something structured and brought to us, packaged and delivered by the ideologues of social science from the United States of America. Secondly, it's a con because it cons us into an easy route to anti-racism, an easy route for those who don't have the courage to face the long march, so to speak. Anti-racism takes us along the path to anti-imperialism; we have to face that. It extends to the communities that we live in and the class to which we belong and which shares our oppressions and exploitations. It is a con too because it deliberately faces us away from the political anti-racist challenges. Finally, it's a con because I think it admits a kind of confessional anti-racism, a kind of band-aid anti-racism alternative to the politics that we're making.

Linton Kwesi Johnson said in one of his poems, describing a black petite bourgeoisie: "They will live off the backs of blacks. They will seek top rates off the backs of blacks".

We have evidence that this obscenity is being elaborated – the privatisation inside the race relations industry. It is obscene and we must not tolerate it. That is why we must bury RAT because it is a diversion from, and a betrayal of, the history of black struggles in this country.

What the street struggles of 1981 were saying wasn't, "We would like you to be more aware of us". We don't want your awareness; we want your action, not awarenes. Racism is being magnified while RAT gets fat. Doesn't this tell you something?

I have one immediate demand. The GLC must take a lead and stop funding RAT. The Council must renounce its support of RAT, particularly since in its enthusiasm and partly out of its confusion it made the error of breathing life into RAT.

Gus John
Manchester Education Department, Race Today Collective

I want to talk from my experience as an education worker in Manchester, but a more lasting experience is that of being part of the education movement of this country since the sixties. Evidence to bury RAT is to be found when we examine what has actually happened with the debate about education and the black community, and particularly the experience of black people within the British education system from 1960-1985. Various local authorities engage in training for all kinds of reasons. They see it as part of class development. Those who take part in it see it as a ticket to career advancement, and if you were to examine some C.V.s these days you would see the number of Racism Awareness Training courses that people have been on which are printed in block capitals on their C.V.s. They see it as a means of enhancing improved practice and that improved practice is generally in the form of legitimising the racism of those institutions themselves. We've got to put the spoke into the whole notion of what training can offer inside of those circles where it is clear that training is being used as a diversion from looking at, laying bare and dealing with the institutional practices of housing departments, education departments and the rest.

I work in a department within a local authority run by a left of centre Labour group which promotes an equal opportunities policy. They made it necessary a couple of years ago for each educational establishment within Manchester to institute something called a policy on racism – IPOR (Institutional Policy on Racism). The vocabulary grows and grows as the industry expands. There is an inspectorate there who drew up an institutional policy on racism using to great benefit the wisdom that they acquired through their Racism Awareness Training. That same inspectorate was responsible for drawing up a curriculum for people between the ages of eleven to sixteen, and if one were to look at the nature of the curriculum and look at what is in that institutional policy on racism, you'll see that the two bear no relevance at all to each other. They are wanting the schools to institute a curriculum which has got all the deficiencies and all the cons that kids in school today are being fed at an alarming rate. In doing that they are actually asking kids not to determine what that curriculum should be; it should have nothing at all to do with the fact of their imminent unemployment; it should have nothing at all to do with what they face on the streets; it should have nothing at all to do with the struggle that their parents, black and white, are waging within the communities, whether it's against the police, against immigration controls, against Norman Tebbitt or whoever else.

It is a sanitised curriculum which does not even take into account the fact that children coming into classrooms come out of a situation in which they are dealing with racism, either as victims or perpetrators, on a day-to-day basis. Yet, their institutional policy on racism talks about getting rid of graffiti in schools that are racist; dealing with racist incidents on the part of white teachers. In other words, sanitising the institutions so that they could continue to oppress black and white young people as if there is no relationship whatsoever between the experiences that they both share. There was a seminar to determine what kind of anti-racist training policy the Education Department should have overall, and it broke up in shambles. The black talkers got together and decided that unless they tell Manchester Education Department how to do anti-racism training then Manchester Education Department should not be allowed to institute an anti-racist training policy. Then there were others who determined that racism is a white problem and those who ought to be dealing with the racism in the white society are white people themselves, so blacks should not be involved in anti-racist training but whites should set up teams of Racism Awareness Training.

In the end Manchester Education Department decided to scrap its original position paper and to invite a consultative exercise with various community groups. There were the usual arguments about whom do you consult. When it was suggested by myself that if they wanted to know who to consult about what to do with racist teachers they should go and ask kids in those schools, they said "No. You can't do that. You cannot go asking kids how to train teachers, it's just not done".

We know the damage that Racism Awareness Training is doing; we know the extent to which it is deflecting from anti-racist, anti-imperialist struggles, and we have to determine that what we do is to block it left, right and centre and organise wherever we are to ensure that it is blocked.

Sabina Sharkey
Irish Anti-Racist Campaigner

We have a history of struggle against racism and against imperialism. It spans over 800 years of the colonisation of Ireland by England, which was entirely effected by its own notion of superiority. They entered a country which had its own civilisation, with its language, customs, judicial system etc. They deemed it "barbaric" and "savage" and attempted to impose their rule on our freedom. Our resistance was a further sign of barbarism and it excused the force and destruction they wrecked upon us. Having exhausted our country's resources, destroyed its trade and reduced the majority of the population to starvation, many Irish were forced to emigrate. The Irish in Britain were readily exploitable cheap labour and inferior human beings within its society, for the reason that they were Irish; the same "inferiority" that allows the British to occupy Ireland against the will of its people to this day.

The connections between the treatment of immigrants in England and the treatment of people in the country from which they emigrated are racist and imperialist connections. This is true of South Africa, of the Caribbean, of India and of Ireland. I am sorry if I seem to labour the point, I only mention it because it brings me to our first criticism of RAT. It chooses to ignore and even deny our history and the similarities in our anti-imperialist, anti-racist struggle and that of black people and ethnic minority people. We are concerned that this is not just an insult to Irish people but to all people engaged in anti-racist, anti-imperialist struggle. For the similarity, despite our differences, in all our struggle is to change the state which through its institutions, laws, and economy, binds us in an oppressive and inferior position. In struggle together, the pressure to make change can be considerable.

But what if the state response is devious? What if instead of tackling the institutional racism it diverts us with small package deals for one or two races, so that we can be pitted against each other, divided or in competition for nothing? And what if they attempt to entice us away from politics with "human awareness" solutions, something to appeal to the human heart? Hence, the development of cheap grant-aid schemes and very expensive RAT, and we are not happy with either.

More specifically we are concerned that there are no anti-racist, anti-imperialist political analysis and political strategies in RAT. Without that we might as well call it human awareness on Mars. Which is probably what makes it so acceptable. Therapy is fine for those who can afford it, but it is no substitute for social change, or for the abolition of a racist state. We would point out that:

(i)   Personal liberation against a backdrop of absolutely unchanging and unchallenged social and political conditions is useless and indulgent.

(ii)   RAT does not deal adequately with issues of responsibility, for if their thesis is that all white people are born racists – then what white person is responsible for their past? – Either they're the inevitable congenital racist or they're that 'much nicer white person:' the anti-racist, again useless in terms of all that needs challenging and changing politically and institutionally.

(iii)   Race Awareness trainers (many of those whom we've dealt with are white British middle-class) like to impress on Irish people that they are not discriminated against, never experience racism and that their history either (a) never happened; or (b) is lies. We wonder in whose interest it is to deny the obvious connections and similarities in our experience and that of the black and other ethnic minority peoples, to deny a whole area of racism, and to pursue the personal to the absolute exclusion of the political?

Plenary discussion

Following the contributions from the Panel members, a number of issues were raised in the ensuing discussion. The main points raised, including rejoinders from the platform, were as follows:

(a)   Racism Awareness Training is a load of rubbish and it's about time people in this room got off their behinds and started doing things to change the structure of this society so that people don't have to live in the kind of fear that they've been living in for about four years. We've got people who have been suffering harassment for sixteen years of their lives and all the Housing Department can say is, "We're not moving them out because we don't want to create any sort of black ghetto in East Ham". Those are the kind of responses that we are getting. What am I supposed to say to those people? I didn't even want to waste my time coming to this conference, and the reason I was late was because there was an arson attack on a Halal meat shop in East Ham and one Asian businessman lost his business and nearly lost his life. I feel humiliated in having to stand up here and justify what black people are suffering. If you don't know what they are suffering, if you can't see with your own eyes. If you can't see what is happening then I don't give a damn about the lot of you. I care about those black people who are suffering and I'll work for those black people and I'll suffer with those black people, and the lot of you can go to hell.

(b)   The converse of this animal called RAT has now been designed for black people to raise their consciousness. Black people are to be lifted out of their internalised oppression and the colonisation of their mind by this training. There is a very strong element of sheer arrogance in this presumption that all of us don't have a clue how racism works and must sit in little groups and be told what we have to do. That can be best done in black political organisations. The implication for black peole who get involved in this RAT for black people is that it teaches them how to extract revenge. That is a mistake, and for that reason there are other ways of raising consc-iousness and forming links which are much better than ideologies.

(c)   I want to change attitudes because I know that the structures of society are such that it is whites who are in the position of decision-making. Those decsion-making whites are informed by certain stereotypes and ideologies which are embedded in British social attitudes. They are not even aware of the fact that they hold those assumptions which are false. Therefore, if Racism Awareness could actually address the issue of seeking to bring out those ideologies and stereotypes then it may have a useful role to play.

    I am opposed to those who would seek to subsume racism and the fight against racism onto a class structure. The reason that I am opposed to it is because black people fall into the same trap that they are accusing other people of. You're telling black people "Look, wait until we have destroyed the class structure then you'll have racial equality". Just like they told us in Africa, "Don't seek the things on this earth, you wait till you die and then God up there will sort things out for you". There is no sign in Britain that a revolution is at hand. And black people have got to wait until you have changed the social structure, until you have brought about revolution, until they can get racial equality? Go and tell those black youngsters on the street who can't get jobs, tell those black people who get the most dilapidated properties that are around that they should wait until you have brought about your revolution. What are you going to use to bring about that revolution? So if you are telling me that I ought to wait until imperialism has been destroyed before I get racial equality I say to hell with you. I want equality no matter what the structure is.

(d)   Everybody here thinks this is the struggle, but the struggle isn't here, it's out on the streets. It's in Newham, it's the Newham Seven, it's all these campaigns – that's the struggle. Something was said about using words like 'middle class', 'intellectual academic', but can't you see that's what RAT has done, it's given all these people the language of oppression and there's no content. There are two positions here. There are those who are saying that racism is about attitude and behaviour as if we were all animals in a zoo and you can come and look at people's behaviour and change them. It's not about that. It's about struggle, it's about the reality of a butcher's shop in Newham being burned down last night; of a pregnant woman with three children being burned out in Ilford. We can do a little thing here today, a little thing. It's not about creating the revolution, but addressing the question, Racism Awareness Training – a part of the problem or part of the solution?

(e)   Racism Awareness Training has functioned as a substitute for campaigning against racism and fascism. As the number of people involved in Racism Awareness Training has gone up, the number of people involved in the anti-fascist struggle has gone down. You take Anti-Racist Year last year, proposals came forward to different councils. Look at the different councils, what was their contribution to Anti-Racist Year? To fund Racism Awareness Training; that was their contribution. You take this conference. This conference is, in fact, just following the same pattern. This is once again another diversion from building an anti-racist movement in this country.

(f)   Sivanandan's article says that Racism Awareness Training is a con because it pretends to move pebbles to move avalanches, but in fact what it does is move pebbles to prevent them. I don't think it has the capacity to cause those avalanches. I don't think it means anything to the structure of this society; it doesn't reveal anything about the capacity of black people outside of those structures; it doesn't have that much influence on us, and frankly I don't see why we should get that heated up about it. In many ways I see a lot of the writings and discussion as really sending your exocet missiles to actually break nuts. I think what we ought to do is to concentrate on our capacity as black people in this society to actually fight racism as we find it and organise so that we can prevent certain measures being taken against us in this society. I really think we ought to take this thing in our stride and in perspective because I don't think it will determine our future here, neither positively or negatively. I think what we ought to do is concentrate on our capacities to fight, to defend, to actually create new spaces for certain things.

Following the discussions, platform speakers were invited to make a final response to the points raised.

Sabina Sharkey

I'm not in a position to make a comprehensive or adequate response to all that was said but there's one point that I would like to clear up – in case there is any misunderstanding. I regret if I gave any cause for misunderstanding, but I thought in what I was saying about the anti-racist and anti-imperialist perspective that we Irish people hold, that it was clear that we are completely behind autonomy of struggle and the rights of us as Irish people and of black people to our own autonomous struggle. What I was trying to say is that in terms of our common experience as well as our different experiences of institutional racism, of racist oppression, of legislative racism, that if we want to change that and the white power structure, there are various ways of doing it and the way that the white middle class like best is where we fragment even over common issues. All I am saying is – we support autonomous struggle entirely, but we also want, as much as possible, to ally with those with whom we are closest in beating common enemies.

Gus John

There are certain things that need to be said. Firstly, there are some very backward notions coming up from contributions which we have, whether we're black or white, to move away from. There is the notion, for example, that to be academic is to be intellectual, is to be detached from struggle or anti-struggle. There is the feeling that if you could snipe at people on the platform whom you identify as academics you dismiss them for all time and dismiss what they have to say as if that bears no relevance whatsoever to the struggles that those people are part of. That is about the most backward notion that I know. I do not believe that in this country the decision that several black people make to join particular sectors of the public service, particularly the public service, is somehow an individualised decision to do with their careers. If you decide to become a policeman you are making a political decision; if you decide to become a probation officer or social worker, you, as a black person, are engaged in a political act based on a political decision, whether you recognise it or not. If you are white and operating within those institutions then you too are saying something about your political selves.

For blacks who are part of Ethnic Minorities Units or Equal Opportunities Units that are mushrooming all over the place because of the new-found wisdom to do with equality and socialism that the Labour Party councils have found, it is imperative that people understand precisely what they are doing and why and where that stands in relation to the struggles that are going on. None of those things have come about in isolation from the struggle that working class black people, young and old, have waged in this society from the time they landed on these shores. We have to understand, therefore, where we stand, where we place ourselves in terms of that sector of struggling working class people in this society. Unless we do that, then we are going to do our best to keep our noses clean and our heads down and not contaminate our careers by engaging in struggle, and deflecting all the time the challenges that are posed to us in these positions by people on whose backs we've got into those situations.

One would have thought that the historic struggle waged by sectors of the black working class, and the youth particularly in this society, would have eclipsed the rising black bourgeoisie. Why, meanwhile, we have to debate RAT and debate the CRE and debate those Ethnic Minorities Units is because those are the instruments by which that same petite bourgeoisie gains the ascendency to do specific things in relation to the struggles waged by black people, and the struggles that ought to have to do with racism are lost. We have to debate those issues and I do not believe that by debating issues, however hotly, one is necessarily fighting amongst ourselves. I deplore the notion that once groups of black people start disagreeing with each other, we are somehow putting paid to some kind of a false unity that in my view is based on smoke, black smoke.

Colin Prescod

Very briefly, we are arguing amongst ourselves in order to get our line right, not because we want to argue and look messy. Secondly, there was some confusion that there appeared to be personal attacks on people. I don't think I've seen that. It's not an attack on the people as persons but on what they do and the effects of what they do; attacks on the practices of people and the effects of those practices. Thirdly, somebody thought that RAT had created jobs. It is not RAT that creates jobs, it is the long struggle that has created the possibility of the openings that exist. Fourthly, there is confusion about what racism is about. Racism is not in service to white psyches nor has it been about making white people feel better and superior.

We talk about class not because all the working-class people, white and black, have some easy unity, but because it helps us to focus on the ruling class that controls the power, in that system. To say class is not to say we resolve anything, it's just to remind us that that is a dimension within which we have to make a struggle. Finally, nobody who was serious about anti-racism and anti-fascism should be concerned about organising on the street, about joining the open courageous struggle against racism and fascism in this society.

Sybil Phoenix

I am proud of the young ones who are taking the struggle on, but before RAT existed the cap was there or the hand was there and Old Hannah has worked so that she has helped with many others to lay the foundation so that now the young ones can take it on. And so the struggle continues.

Pamela Nanda

We are trained all our lives, one way or another, by a school, by parents or whatever, and today there has been a unanimous feeling about Racism Awareness Training. One of the questions from the floor was whether we denounced training as such, totally and completely, and if we don't, if we are talking about organising, about support, about whatever that's been talked about this morning, is how that training works and how we move it away from and what Siva called 'burying the RAT'.

Ahmed Gurnah

Not so long ago this kind of discussion probably wouldn't have taken place, and it is wrong to think that it isn't important because over the years, in various ways things like RAT have appeared. There's been other things in the past, and they get killed and then they reappear again. This kind of discussion is ensuring that not only do we bury RAT, but we make sure that we don't bury the undead.

Afternoon Session

The discussions at the various workshops were reported back to a plenary session. The main points of these sessions were as follows:

Workshop 1:

An Alternative to Racism Awareness Training

A number of points were discussed and a number of perspectives put forward. First of all, a general point about the discussion tended to be in terms of alternative training strategies to Racism Awareness Training. The point was raised, though, on a number of occasions, that, given the scarce resources which are available to pursue anti-racist work, whether or not any money should go to training at all. That money could, in fact, be spent in terms of support to black self-help. Talking about training, a number of points were put forward. Some involved training for black and other ethnic minorities-based organisations in order that they could be better equipped to operate. Some training could go towards newly recruited black and ethnic minority staff coming into an organisation, particularly in cases where staff were being recruited who didn't have "formal qualifications" but were expected to do a specific job of work. Training for trainers was another way in which training would be used, there again to help equip black people newly arrived in an organisation to come to grips with that organisation and not to get swamped within it. Training to build on the implementation of policies was put forward, and of the various types of training which were discussed this seems to be the one which should be given priority.

The need to monitor training was emphasised, particularly the need to look at training within the context of other things. The question of how far training could bring about change was also raised, and the fact that in a number of organisations training in terms of race was often being used as a means to try and bring about much wider and more fundamental changes within an organisation, changes which should have been occurring anyway. Yet again, an increased burden was being placed on black and ethnic minority people to bring about changes which should have been happening through political activity in a wider sense.

Workshop 2:

A Critical Appraisal of Racism Awareness Training

There was an argument in our group at first because some people wanted to adopt a critical approach towards Racism Awareness Training without taking in race and class, but there was a vote and eventually three or four people left. Some members of our group expressed a view that they didn't really regard the critiques that were advanced this morning as being adequate. They felt that some people wanted to know exactly what type of Racism Awareness Training there was, and some members of the group pointed out that there was one sort of trainer, the individual orientated type, which is a hangover from American psychotherapy, and there is another type of Racism Awareness Training which looks at institutional aspects and the way structures operate to oppress black people. People were questioning the whole notion that Racism Awareness Training necessarily needed to be psychologistic. There were various other questions raised. Some people felt that the only way to evaluate Racism Awareness Training was whether or not it actually served to help black people in their struggle, and there were disputes about that. Some people said that it was important in the sense that quite often it did provide a forum for initial discussion on racism, and that in deep-seated white organisations that were totally unaware of the fact that there were actually black people in this country you did need something to actually initiate discussion.

Some people felt that the approach of some of the speakers today was a little unfair to quite a lot of the black action that's occurring, and felt that it wasn't necessarily fair to take black action as just one line. The struggle took many forms and was going to take many different roads, and simply to talk about it purely in terms of class struggle wasn't correct. Some people also said that the central assumption of Racism Awareness Training, that prejudice plus power equals racism, isn't actually correct. It was said that racism is a lot more specific – it's about virginity tests at Heathrow, oppression at a work place, and many other more down-to-earth things. Somebody did point out that we should be aware that in South Africa, after Racism Awareness Training was instigated, about 1,000 black groups were created, so that is was important to see that it could have, through some weird sort of an effect, a knock-on consequence for black political action.

The central feeling was that Racism Awareness Training wasn't any good, but if it was going to be used it should concentrate more on institutional racism, though not neglect the fact that it's individuals that are racist. It was felt that you can't neatly divorce an individual from the structure the individual is in, and that sometimes to just talk about things in that way is incorrect. Three main proposals were made:

(a)   The workshop strongly urges the GLC to refrain from funding RAT courses and to discontinue the present funding as soon as possible.

(b)   Monies allocated by the GLC's Ethnic Minorities Unit for RAT should be used to fund community organisations to unite the black struggle.

(c)   Racism Awareness Training ought to take place only in the context of, and as an integral part of, a specific anti-racist programme of work designed to illuminate racist discrimination within organisational structures and bring about racial equality.

Workshop 3:

Problems in Running a Racism Awareness Unit

Quite a lot of issues came out in our workshop but we weren't able to thrash out everything because of the time we had. In our group, we had two trainers and also people who have been involved in Racism Awareness Training, and the first thing that came out was that in running a Racism Awareness Workshop you always have to consider the other 'isms', such as sexism, and the class issue. What came out of, say, the class issue is that when you have a workshop on Racism Awareness Training and the class issue is discussed, black people are not included as part of the class system. Another thing that always comes up in Racism Awareness Training is that Irish and Jewish people suffer from racism.

Consideration was then given to whether or not the facilitators who do Racism Awareness Training should be black or white. The consensus was that it's fair that both black people and white people should do it; the black being the one who is being oppressed, and the white who is the oppressor.

Another thing that came out was, where do trainers get their training? The consensus on that was it would be a good idea for all trainers to meet, to look at their training and the training that they are giving to people. People are saying "What is Racism Awareness Training?", and I think what it came down to was Racism Awareness Training is actually about breaking down negative images that white people have of black people, and also the negative images that black people themselves may have internalised. Another thing that came up was that there is not enough visual material on Racism Awareness Training available. Another question that was asked was "Is Racism Awareness Training enough?" A trainer in the workshop said that she had two separate groups – one for a white group, which she calls Racism Awareness Training, but another one for black people which she doesn't see as Racism Awareness Training, but Black Awareness Training.

Workshop 4:

A Positive approach to Racism Awareness Training in Education

A discussion took place on how to get Racism Awareness Training introduced in education. It was pointed out that the issue of racism should be dealt with in courses on the mainstream curriculum, and not marginalised. Section 11 funding, it was argued, marginalises the education of black children into special units and has no effect on the mainstream attitudes. A recommendation was made that anti-racist training should be introduced in all teacher training courses, not as a module, but as an integral part of the syllabus. However, this was considered to be only a part of the solution since the trainers themselves do not receive any kind of training.

Workshop 5:
Race Advisors and Black Struggle

The main strand of argument in our workshop was, what is it we are struggling against? This is the sort of definition that race advisors should first of all sort out. Is it to become equal with white people on their terms, their definition, within the same racist structures and power base? Where does an advisor's accountability lie? Does it lie with the kids in the streets, or in the institutions? What is the black perspective? What is the black struggle at all levels – jobs, housing, education?

People in an advisory capacity in equal opportunity and race advisory jobs are in danger of listening to white definitions of black political struggle. They need to become actively involved in the campaigns of the community and black political struggle. They should be pushing for black studies, black history, and taking this into the workplace, manipulating their roles and positions and getting their roles established, not necessarily as advisors but working within a corporate political structure responding to the black political power base which is staring us in the eyes, rather than use the myth that we have no power base, no economic base or black perspective. Advisors should connect black workers at all levels in their institutions and become organised. They are there to be accountable to the community. In other words, they should be seen as working there for the black cause and not just to develop other staff or other institutions.

Workshop 6:
Racism Awareness Training and Women's Oppression

I think this is quite interesting, that most of the people who are reporting back are women which is very different to how it was this morning. I must say that I was feeling quite oppressed this morning. Although I was feeling angry at a lot of things which were being said, I didn't feel that I could come up here and make any comment on that because the majority of people who were making statements were men and doing it in their totally aggressive way as some men do.

We talked about the plenary session this morning which we felt didn't really look at the many different types of Racism Awareness Training courses which are available. The differences were not actually clarified and very little was said about anti-racist training courses, rather than Racism Awareness Training courses. I think there is a difference.

It is assumed that Racism Awareness Training tries to change individuals, and we feel that trainers or facilitators actually take people through experiential sessions so they become aware of the different views or different interpretations of certain things, and it is up to the individuals themselves to take responsibility as regards to the sort of work they would then do as a result of the learning processes which they experience. There was also concern about the fact that when Racism Awareness Training was being talked about, the view was expressed that after an individual has done a course, he or she should become anti-racist there and then. This type of expectation is not held for other types of training which people undertake.

There was also concern that in the discussion on Racism Awareness Training, people didn't actually say much about the courses organised by black advisors and local authorities, for instance, for black workers, and the positive gains that these black people got once they've undertaken the training. The morning session implicitly viewed Racism Awareness Training purely for white workers and we felt that the area of training or the benefits gained by black workers themselves was also positive and something that people ought to be expanding.

We had two people who had recently undertaken Racism Awareness Training and had had positive experiences, and in fact came to this conference today to see how they could build on these positive experiences which they had gained as a result of their undertaking that training. Unfortunately, the discussion this morning actually rendered them totally confused and paralysed.

Workshop 7:
Imperialism and Racism and the Irish Perspective

I've just got four brief points. The first point was that we wanted the GLC to set up a forum to counteract imperialism and racism for community groups within London. This could be done by the GLC organising a conference, or otherwise it could be organised by the community groups themselves. In terms of the Irish community we wanted the GLC to take steps to fully examine race discrimination against Irish people, especially in terms of its own employment policy. Quite a number of councils and the GLC are talking a lot about racism while ignoring the fact that there are very few Irish people employed within the GLC and within local councils. It's okay to do jobs as labourers or chambermaids, but don't let them into positions of power.

It was felt too within the group that Racism Awareness Training doesn't acknowledge that racism was reared in imperialist colonisation and as such has value to the Irish experience. It was interesting that the GLC put Irish groups within their white European category. After something like 800 years of colonisation and imperialism they link us up with Europe.

Any successor to Racism Awareness Training should concentrate on establishing parallels and building links between oppressed people to strengthen the anti-racist and anti imperialist struggles.

It was felt quite strongly in our group that people should learn from each other's experiences and to build up links together because if we divide and rule we're just playing the capitalist game.

Fitzroy Ambursley

Before closing the conference can I just repeat what I said this morning. This was a consultation exercise. We did want to hear from the community its views about Racism Awareness Training. The reason why it would have seemed that the panel in particular was slanted in favour of those who were critical of Racism Awareness Training was precisely because people who are firm supporters of it were not prepared to come and speak on the panel. A number of prominent people who are involved in Racism Awareness Training, including one person who is here today, refused point blank to come on the panel, so I think it is their responsibility if this morning's session took the form that it took.

Appendix A

The Politics of Racism Awareness Training

Ahmed Gurnah
Department of Applied Social Studies
Sheffield City Polytechnic

I want to thank Ashok Ohri, Phil Lee, Pete Ashworth and Trev Phelps for commenting on the manuscript. I am also grateful to Bisi Williams, Alison Davis and Bruce Senior for discussing these issues with me at length. But I am most grateful to Rosie Betterton and Anil Gupta for their most valuable advice. They all helped to moderate my natural imprudence.

Abstract

In less than five years, Racism Awareness Training (RAT) has established itself the reputation of being the crucial and the most practical initial step against personal and institutional racism. In this discussion, I wish to examine its assumptions, strategy and action and to register my doubts about its success. Furthermore, I shall suggest that RAT can have dubious side-effects which somewhat divert people from taking positive action.

Introduction

In the last five years, especially since the summer 1981 black rebellions, Racism Awareness Training has come to be for many in the public and private services, a small but crucial step against racism. Its success is evident by the regard in which it is held by many progressive local authorities, social services departments, schools, colleges, polytechnics, hospitals, banks and even by some sections of the state. At a conference held in London on 21 March 1984, on "Local Authorities and Racial Disadvantage", David Waddington, a Home Office minister responsible for deportation and immigration controls, agreed that staff and management skills should be developed using Racism Awareness Training, with the chief officers taking the lead. A document published by the Department of the Environment, issued as a *Report of a Joint Government and Local Authority Association Working Group,* also states its commitment to "race relations training". This training, it insists, is required to be given to "elected Members" and to local authority officers, who must be made aware of their role as employers during selection and recruitment and while providing social services. Training should also be made available to the black staff "to enable them to progress within the authority". Because:

> *"other than in fairly specialist areas, there is a substantial unmet training need which just a few authorities are developing strategies to tackle."* [1]

In this document, the *Working Group* report approvingly on various initiatives taken by councils like Bradford and Nottingham which is "developing racism awareness courses for staff, starting with top management", while Newham "has used a variety of approaches including experiential techniques and games" to pursue their objectives. Northamptonshire, Coventry, Lambeth and Haringey too have related initiatives. The feeling of the *Working Group* was that training programmes should cover "two main areas – awareness training and training related to policy and practice". [2] Indeed, they noted that even the Police:

> *"had put some effort into the field of awareness training and it was felt that such training was especially important in ensuring key people in a position to influence policy and practice realised the need for positive action and for attitudes to change".* [3]

The report recognised the immediate need to concentrate on the "needs of senior personnel and elected members", because they are involved with external matters. [4] Bradford clearly understanding this, planned to ensure that at least one member of "any group engaged in the selection of employees" has received such training. This council hopes that:

> *"By 1985, half of any such group will have to be trained. By 1986, no member or officer will be allowed to take part in selection of employees*

unless he has received equal opportunity training." [5]

Thus, as a response to racism, many councils including Brent, Lewisham, Camden, Sheffield, Liverpool, Greater Manchester, Leicester and the GLC, have set up Race Relations Units or ethnic minority units. The majority of these units have understood their brief as that of training; and have chosen RAT as the best method of training. As the Haringey Community Affairs Committee Report insists, training is essential for providing "a service to our multi-ethnic community" and "to eliminate personal and institutional discrimination".

"Racism Awareness Training should be central to all race relations training in order that staff can approach the issues facing them with more awareness and confidence". [6]

It is obvious why such training should appeal to so many people. Essentially, RAT is concerned with **practical** problems. It appears to address racism not only at the state and institutional level, as do most political activists and academic sociologists, but it is also **rightly** concerned with people's personal experiences of racism. Particularly after the summer 1981 black rebellions, we cannot over-estimate the appeal of practical solutions to institutional and personal racism. Such solutions attract many interests.

Firstly, they attract black people because to some of them RAT seems to force the recognition of their oppression on the establishment and on the professional middle class; but more importantly, it appears to constitute a concrete programme against that oppression. Secondly, RAT solutions allure parts of the liberal establishment because they provide an answer to their moral opposition to racism. Thirdly, various individuals too are drawn to these solutions because they promise to clear up their confusions and uncertainties about racism. For many, RAT appears to reveal to them extremely important facts about themselves and about their racist society. Finally, even the racist state is persuaded that such training and a better trained police force is bound to increase law and order.

It is hoped that training would sensitise and stimulate the professional imagination to the extent of motivating action against racism at work, at home and socially. For many people, then, if RAT does not provide a simple solution to the struggle against racism, it certainly amounts to modest steps in that direction. At the very least, RAT has brought many blacks into prominence as trainers, to question and to influence community work decisions, social work practice, teaching curricula and methods, recruitment and selection procedures, employment policies and so on. RAT has given blacks a positive image, ensured some black jobs as trainers, and has created an atmosphere of confidence for black workers, and the possibility of promotion for some black workers.

These are powerful factors to recommend RAT. There is no reason for anyone to be dismissive of their importance, especially if what trainers and many who have been on the course claim is true: that it does make a difference. But however much RAT widely appeals to the professional middle class, to blacks, to the state, it has never really been placed, or placed itself, in a critical context. This discussion will address itself to that end. But first let us see what RAT is all about.

Racism Awareness Training

As indicated, RAT is not interested in theoretical concerns, but is mainly preoccupied with practical ones. That is both its strength and weakness. It is its strength because it addresses a wider range of people and better appeals to their concerns. It is its weakness because it rarely reflects on the consequences of its assumptions and actions. Nevertheless, in as much as RAT is informed by theory, it appears to be underpinned by two theoretical frameworks: Marxist sociology and Rogerian social psychology. However, these two theoretical frameworks are not evaluated within the context of training, they merely presuppose training: Marxism and Rogerian psychology are used as slogans. Therefore, it would be inaccurate to call RAT either "Marxist" or "Rogerian". because as theories they are of no interest to the trainers: their usage is entirely pragmatic. One reason why they reappear in numerous RAT articles is that they appeared in the influential Judy Katz and Allen Ivey article "White Awareness: The Frontier of Racism Awareness Training", and in Katz's book *White Awareness*.

These theories have very specific explanatory roles to play in the make-up of RAT. Marxism helps to identify and describe institutional and individual racism. Rogerian psychology outlines the way racism affects individuals and also provides a practical method for dealing with racism, through the individual. Since neither the choice of these theories nor the relationship between them is ever theorised in RAT, they remain as slogans. They are arbitrarily selected for their convenience, without care about whether they are properly understood or whether their implications are in concert with the aims of training. They are treated as simple convenient tools for identifying and for taking action against racism. Theory stops being a form of reflection and becomes a technique. But, if Katz and Ivey fail to theorise the relationship because of the two frameworks and the consequences of using them, many of their British followers are not even aware that they have been presupposed. For them, RAT is simply a technique against racism. Further still, many of these followers would openly dispute the necessity for **any** theoretical reflection, arguing that training must be kept at the level of feeling.

(a) *Marxist sociological approach:* describing racism

Judy Katz sets the scene in the following material fashion, by insisting that racism is:

> *"the racial prejudice of white people coupled with the economic, political, and social power to enforce discriminatory practices on every level of life – cultural, institutional and individual".* [7]

From this she concludes that in the United States, the "race problem" is "essentially a white problem in that whites (who) developed it, perpetuated it, and have power to resolve it...", by establishing "policies and practices that serve to their advantage and benefit..." [8] But these policies and practices" are neither described nor analysed. In fact, the whole "analysis" takes up no more than a few pages of the whole book, which is mostly a training manual.

Antoinette Satow of the *Racism Awareness Programme Unit (RAPU)* reproduces a version of Katz's construction when she says:

> *"Since the time when racism became accepted to the material advantage of white society, the history of white people is one of participating in oppressive relationships with black people. Racism has become embedded in the ideology, policies and structures of institutions, and has invidiously distorted the thinking and expectations of individuals."* [9]

Due to similar sociological and historical considerations, Basil Manning and Ashok Ohri [10] reject multi-culturalism in the form of "race relations" politics. For them, like for many other radical blacks, race relations assumes racial equality and racial harmony. It implies "multi-racial festivals...multi-racial playmates...(and) in the belief that if different races mix together and 'understand each other'", that this would remove tensions and demonstrate to "the NF that black and white can live in harmony". But the fact is, they continue, none of this is possible without "racial justice". Therefore, it will not do to encourage white community workers to believe that all they need to do against racism is to learn about black cultures and life styles. Then "'the victims' become equated with 'the problem'". [11] The colonial context of black and white people and the contemporary institutional and individual acculturation of white people, turns the latter into racists. The process of undoing this complex and endemic relationship is extremely difficult and it has not, indeed it cannot, be achieved by liberal measures of race relations politics.

Fighting racism is particularly difficult in this context, they continue, because in spite of pervasive institutional and individual racism in Britain, public service workers have little notion of how to deal with it. Manning and Ohri are concerned that racist socialisation renders professional bodies "afraid to articulate possible ways of addressing it". For, in order to challenge racism we must "understand the dynamics of racism". [12]

"The task is to identify issues that can demonstrate the hidden working of racism in the state services and other institutions". [13]

Neutrality is no solution either. To fail to acknowledge black oppression is to be a "non-racist racist". It is to "vote for status quo". [14] Where this happens, it is impossible to either evaluate collusion or challenge racism.

"It becomes unsafe for any one to raise the issue of racism in an honest, self-critical and constructive way...believing themselves to be committed anti-racist, but fearing to put that to the test"... [15]

For these reasons, RAT conceives of racism as a white problem, because it is socialised into white institutions and white individuals. In this way also, Manning and Ohri, like many other British trainers, correctly distance themselves from liberal "race awareness training" or multi-culturalism.

(b) *The social psychological approach:*
the psychological effects of racism

The second theoretical slogan adopted by RAT originates from American social psychology and is only cosmetically connected to Marxism: that is, there is no theoretical continuity from the one to the other. Rogerian distinction is made between the actual (racist) and the ideal (non-racist or anti-racist) self-concept. According to Judy Katz and Allen Ivey, racism distorts people's conceptions of reality so much that it creates an internal conflict both for the racist and for the "victim" of racism. They approvingly quote Gunnar Myrdal's observation that the "American ideals of equality, freedom, God-given rights on the one hand" are in pathological conflict with "practices of discrimination, humiliation, insult, denial of opportunities to Negroes...in a racist society on the other". [16]

The outcome of this internal conflict, continue Katz and Ivey, is mental illness for both blacks and whites. When whites fail to acknowledge these internal conflicts by either intellectually or institutionally rationalising them, these conflicts only reappear in the shape of increased racist attitude and behaviour. That in turn for Katz and Ivey, leads to greater damage in white people's mental health, in their marital and work relations.

"People who avoid and deny their role in perpetuating and maintaining racism may also deny the reality of true relationships between

husband and wife, between parent and child, between employer and employees". [17]

It looks like several analytical jumps are being made here. As well as the jump from racism to mental illness, there is a leap from racism to sexual oppression, to child oppression and to class oppression. The connections, if they exist, are not demonstrated, they are simply stated. Perhaps such connections do exist, but except for a few vague references, no arguments are offered to establish their legitimacy.

In addition to these analytical leaps, Katz's and Ivy's appropriation and usage of their version of the Rogerian notion of actual and ideal self-concept implies a metaphysical conception of an ideal person. Oppression is said to affect ideality of personal existence and creates a pathology in it, but no sound reasons are given why people should become mentally disturbed simply because they are racist, sexist or bourgeois exploiters. Nor are there any arguments rehearsed which show that the effect of racism, sexism and class exploitation on blacks, women and the working-class is to make them mentally disturbed. The only implied reason that one can detect from a very brief discussion by Katz and Ivey, is that these oppressions offend the ideal person, the essential person. For it is only when one adheres to such a metaphysical notion of person, which implies a basic human nature, that one can introduce notions of mental disturbances if their essential nature is confounded. If what they say is meant simply to suggest (as Rogers does) that ideal self-conception implies an easy-going pragmatic existentialist humanism, then, there would be no need to either imply metaphysics or mental sickness. In that case racism would merely disgruntle people, because it blocks them from achieving their ideality.

Not only are RAT's assumptions, as represented by Katz and Ivey, theoretically inadequate and metaphysical, they are also reductionist in the extreme. RAT implies that people experience all oppressions in the same way, because all social oppressions arise, or at least are exacerbated, by racism. This reduction becomes an absurdity when it also implies that racism mentally affects blacks and whites in the same way. What the evidence in fact suggests, is that racism not only affects blacks and whites differentially, but it also affects different groups of blacks according to their cultural, class, educational backgrounds. Indeed, the evidence shows that when stress is applied, different individuals, partly in accordance with social development and partly due to personal biography, cope with it accordingly. Similarly the way that blacks resist racism or individually counter it, differs according to these factors. For example, there is a great deal of difference in the way that an Asian business man responds and counters racism from the way that an

Asian woman, or an Afro-Caribbean youth (say a Rastafarian), or an Afro-Caribbean mother, or an Asian youth might do it. Very few of these blacks become mentally disturbed simply because they experience racism or because of the strategies they adopt against it. In fact, quite contrary to that, not only do different groups experience and cope with racism in different ways, but increasingly instead of going mad, their experience becomes a basis for black collective action against racism. Indeed, there is a lot of evidence to indicate that black mental illness itself is something of a racist construct. [18] To suggest, as do Katz, Ivey and Satow, that the majority of white people are mentally disturbed because they are racists, surely deserves some evidence. However, untroubled by these concerns, Katz and Ivey continue:

"the disease of racism runs deeply through every white citizen...because reality is distorted when one is mentally ill, there is difficulty in coping with reality." [19]

The evidence in fact points to a contrary view. Those who have racial gender and class-power, distorted or not, are usually the ones who have psychological and material resources to deal **better** with reality; they control it. Unless reality too is conceived of as a metaphysical entity, as an ideal state, the people who have no control of it are usually not the oppressors, but the oppressed. They have no control of it not because their minds are distorted, but because they are denied access to those resources. For indeed reality is neither just a mental experience nor an ideal metaphysical blob out there; it is a lived experience of access to power and social, cultural, economic and physical resources.

Thus, what at first appeared to be a theoretical underpinning of the practice of Racism Awareness Training now looks like a scissors and paste job. The most serious problem of the RAT framework is, it depends on definitions, where no connection is made between those definitions and racism. Racism is said to be "prejudice plus power", as self evident truth, not as something that needs to be demonstrated. Though at first sight this formula appears useful, various difficulties arise as soon as one starts to probe it. For example, when blacks have prejudice and power, does that make them racist? Does it mean that everytime a powerful white dislikes a black person, that this is racist? What if a powerful white man dislikes a black man because of the perfume the black wears, does this make the white a racist? What if the same white man despises a black woman because of her gender? How could Katz explain a working-class white woman's disdain for a middle-class black woman? How do we explain prejudiced behaviour of a powerful black leader in the West or in the Third World? There is no reflection on any of these matters, instead RAT depends on a series of other definitions like "Britain is a multi-racial society", "racism is a white problem",* "racism is a white professional problem"; we are also given various definitions of racism, ethnocentricism, anti-racism etc. But these kinds definitions are not only problematic because they are imprecise, but because they are also extremely superficial.

Secondly, the absence of theoretical reflection allows RAT to hold conflicting frameworks such as Marxism and Rogerian psychology without noticing the disjuncture. It also permits illegitimate analytical leaps to be made from descriptions of a capitalist phenomena to descriptions of psychological rationalisations. Then, further jumps are made from that to metaphysical assumptions of a balanced person and a static reality.

Thirdly, the absence of written material on RAT philosophy and on discussions about the theoretical and practical difficulties facing trainers and the trained and so on, is itself very suggestive. Apart from it suggesting lack of reflection, it may imply the poverty of RAT philosophy. Most of these theoretical difficulties are reproduced in the RAT strategy.

The Strategy of Racism Awareness Training: **Therapy**

The strategy of RAT also originates from American social psychology, as a simplified version of Carl Roger's work. Whether trainers are conscious of it or not (Katz is conscious of it and her British followers are not) Rogerian therapy, especially his Q sorts, provides a crucial basis on which RAT makes links between its analysis and its strategy against racism. As Katz and Ivey

---

* *It was once suggested to me that the difficulties of this statement becomes most obvious when one applies it to women. For example, if a man approached a feminist and said: "Sexism is a male problem, leave it to me"!*

understand them, Q sorts measure and clarify "distinctions between self and ideal self-concept". By resolving the "discrepancy which arises between the actual and the ideal self-concepts, between structural reality and personal perception, they hope to cure racism. [20] But since racism distorts social reality for all, including the trainers and counsellors, action against racism has to also recognise that the educator must be educated too. Otherwise the "act of counselling and helping will consist only of empty myths". [21] But once the counsellor is trained, he or she can help white people deal with their reality. But the job is a difficult one:

> *"The disease of racism manifests itself in a tremendous degree of pain, guilt, and fear for white people. The discrepancy creates guilt...immobilisation and feeling sorry for oneself".* [22]

It leads to identity confusion. It makes white Americans and Britons adhere to their **national** identity and deny their whiteness; that prevents them "from becoming a fully developed and whole person". Thus, "we must begin to remove the intellectual shackles and psychological chains that keep us in mental bondage. White people have been hurt too long". [23] Similarly, let a man dare suggest to a feminist that he had suffered too long from sexism!

A few analytical jumps are evident here too. For instance, it is not documented how extensive is the white guilt, or how it manifests itself. We are not given the evidence to show us who feels the pain. It is not explained how whites can continue to have political, economic, cultural and social power when they are so immobilised by racism. We are left to wonder why their distorted perception does not make whites more vulnerable and compel them to relinquish their privileges. Racism which had initially been described in historical slogans, now appears in terms of colour. People are said to be racist because they opt for a **national** rather than a colour identity. It seems puzzling that Katz and Ivey should so bitterly lament the **white** suffering of racism.

The material point, however, is that whites should be confronted with their discrepancies, to help them define racism as a white problem:

> *"to raise the consciousness of white people, help them to identify racism in their experience...to take action against institutional and individual racism".* [24]

Furthermore, many of the black trainers in Britiain emphasise the importance of doing similar training with black people, so that blacks can independently put pressure on the white professionals. There are some trainers who insist that training should be conducted only by blacks. But all agree that racism in the first place, should be confronted via RAT.

What is problematic with most of this analysis is that it is too superficial and static. Is assumes that by "defining" the problem, one can also "define" a solution. What is profoundly mistaken about the slogan, "**racism is a white problem**" is that it fails to recognise that racism is a **relationship.** In a relationship one cannot fruitfully focus on the **nature** of the individual in the hope of solving structural inequalities. There is no direct causal route from the nature of the individual and structural dynamics. The analyses **and** the political action by necessity has to address the structural components themselves, and reflect on the individual only in that context. RAT, however, hopes to solve these social inequalities by persuading professionals to recognise their personal racism. The professionals are then expected to translate their raised consciousness into action against institutional racism. They propose to do this, according to Katz and Ivey, in twenty-six hours of intensive Racism Awareness Training, and RAPU can do it only in twenty hours.

It is no part of this argument to imply that these trainers are necessarily cynical or that they lack integrity or seriousness. Quite the contrary, for the most part the people involved in conducting such training are highly committed and many are black. The point that this discussion should convey, is that the lack of theoretical reflection on their part, has landed them in many unintended difficulties. These difficulties become more acute when one probes further into the politics of Racism Awareness Training.*

The Politics of Racism Awareness Training: Some general criticisms

In many ways, though extremely important, the textual criticisms made so far may be of much more interest to professional sociologists than to people who are looking for practical problems. If that were all that was problematic about RAT, one cannot then blame trainers if they chose to ignore these criticisms. Unfortunately, however, even more damaging criticisms can be made about RAT practice. These criticisms come under four general discussion areas. 1. Criticisms connected with the **tone** of RAT; 2. Criticisms to do with the **consequences** of RAT; 3. Criticisms which identify RAT as misdirected energy; and 4. Criticisms about the **ethics** of RAT. By no means do all trainers necessarily exhibit all these characteristics in the same way or to the same extent.

---

* I refrain from discussing the techniques of training, which include group work and role playing and therapy. For if I open up that discussion, I would also need to make a detailed critique of social psychological techniques and that would drift a little too far from our focus. Besides, these arguments are already extensively rehearsed (see footnote 18).

1. The Tone of Racism Awareness Training

The tone of RAT is often accusatory and appears to put people on the spot, in order that they may confront themselves. In this sense, it is highly moralistic. Sometimes, what RAT lacks in content, it makes up in high-mindedness. A particularly extreme, but also revealing example of that tone, is Tuku Mukherjee's "I am not blaming you". But the title is deceptive, for he very soon states "I am not the problem. You are". [25]

> *"Given the context of relationships, splitting up homes and kids (I am not blaming you) given the process your white socialisation, given the ideological forces which are impacting throughout your life; there is no way you have escaped racial prejudice...The code by which I live life...That is your white liberal creation...Your racism has been your silence".* [26]

Even if Mukherjee is right about what he says, it is doubtful that he needs to adopt such a personal note. Furthermore, his approach gives the impression that his critique is not so much of a racist structure which envelops us all, but it is the creation and the responsibility of the white social services workers of Tooting. In spite of all his protestations to the contrary, he is clearly blaming **them.** "I will never forget my 21 jobs. I don't want to hold that against you. The day I forget that experience I've had it." [27]

Now, clearly not all the trainers are as accusative as this, but given the objectives and the method that RAT has chosen to achieve its aims, the even more restrained trainers in the end are incriminating. For the objective of this kind of discussion can only be to guilt-trip the white workers into action against racism. This disposition is very well exemplified by Ruddell and Simpson [28] in their concept of the anti-racist/racist. For them this concept implies that when whites mobilise against racism by giving money and time, or when they join in initiatives to improve black prospects in housing provision, employment, civil rights, schooling and recreations, or when whites fight racist political, economic, and cultural oppressions, the most they can be is anti-racist/racists. RAT's political theory, then, is the tendencey to taunt white people. The implication is that whites must be made to feel and accept their guilt, whatever else they actually do. This approach is mistaken because individual guilt rarely leads to positive action; and then, it is unclear that even if it did, that would constitute the right kind of action.

Thus, if whites cannot possibly by-pass or overcome their guilt and their responsibility for racism, they can alleviate their situation by admitting to it in a pentecostal fashion, by showing that they repent. As Katz and Ivey point out, those who "avoid and deny their role in perpetuating and maintaining racism" and "claim innocence" saying..."I am not racist...I have black friends..(and deny that) racism is a white problem..." [29] are in the end just sick. Thus RAT depends on, nay demands that people doing these sessions must **confess** their racism. For not to do that is held as clear evidence of their refusal to admit that racism is a white problem, and signals their failure to recognise the discrepancy between liberal democratic ideals of equality and justice and the racism they perpetrate on blacks. Brenda Thompson provides an excellent example of repentance in two short articles "Racism Awareness Rules - OK?" and "I am a White Racist – but willing to learn". She says in the second:

"This is a personal look at racism and ethnocentricism which I am discovering in myself and gradually, sometimes painfully, learning to transcend". [30]

When she was young, she was raised to be British. But when in Nigeria, her husband discovered Chinua Achebe and she discovered different ways of raising and carrying her child; this made her aware of ethnocentricism. From the Nigerians she learnt a lot about imperialism and "racism of the colonised".

In "Racism Awareness Rules – OK?", she describes her transformation from "a liberal loving, accepting" mother, to an anti-racist and to her awareness of herself as a white.

"increasingly...I realise that I cannot divorce myself from them and imagine that my own whiteness, my very language and the thought patterns it conveys, were not a contributory part. I was the closest and the most readily objectifiable representation of the pain of the endemic racism of our society..." [31]

Brenda Thompson is quite right to make all these connections between her western socialisation and racism. But is does seem to be rather unhelpful that she should blame it on herself.

But RAT is not only guilt-trips whites, it also affects blacks who get involved with it. The whole atmosphere of recantation encourages blacks to play their part in this unseemly performance. Some RAT for blacks actually teaches blacks the techniques for extracting such behaviour from well-meaning, guilt-ridden whites like Brenda Thompson. It also has a tendency to render discourse extremely **precious,** where both trainers and trained talk in hushed sincere voices about their search for the inner meaning of their feelings; the inner feelings of their racism. Thus, in its tone at least, RAT is highly dubious.

2. Negative Consequences of Racism Awareness Training

RAT has negative consequences because it is based on a non-reflective framework, but more serious than that, because it provides white officials with the acceptable language of anti-racism, with which to disarm black criticisms. There is nothing more disarming to a black person than a powerful official humbly declaring his or her institutional and personal racism upfront, especially when she/he promises to do something about it. It is reminiscent of men's groups, where men can learn the correct language with which to cope with feminists they know. Thus, instead of achieving the required transformation of racist thought and behaviour, RAT may very well unintentionally encourage tokenism.

In the last analysis, the only real measure of anti-racist success is a concrete transformation of black people's conditions in Britain. However, in the last three years during which RAT has been increasing its activities, what is noticeable is the increase of state racism (e.g. Nationality Bill, Police Bill) and the denial of basic bourgeois democratic rights to blacks. There has similarly been a proportional increase of black unemployment and of deteriorating educational facilities. The impression is that state institutions are still not significantly responding to the criticism of racism, but display the ability to "manage" these criticisms, and better "cope" with blacks making them. Clearly RAT has been instrumental in setting up some jobs in some authorities, but this has tended to be in order to achieve the aforementioned requirements.

The state has well anticipated the possibility of further black rebellions. It has strengthened, equipped and trained a bigger police force; it has increasingly encouraged multi-culturalism in schools and public services, and finally (ironically) it has diverted legitimate black and white opposition to state and institutional racism by sending or approving the sending of a few public officials on RAT.* In these ways, the Police, multi-culturalism and RAT are used by the central and the local state to manage blacks.**

Thus, instead of spending the scarce resources set aside for anti-racism on young blacks, on community centres, on creating employment, some local authorities waste a good chunk of the little enough resources on (at

---

* *Some such officials were sent to the American Air Force Base at Alconbury, where they experienced what some American soldiers had to learn, to more effectively defeat the Vietnamese.*
***John Fernandes certainly experienced it in this way. Soon after he was sacked from Hendon Police College for publishing cadets' racist essays. Fernandes alleges that the Police brought in Racism Awareness Programme Unit (RAPU) who went, in spite of advice to the contrary from Fernandes.*

worst) camouflaging the issues, or (at best) on providing a few jobs for blacks.

3. Misdirected Energies

Thus, in spite of the intention to fight institutional racism, it is doubtful that the best way to do that is by individually persuading the various officials. These public officers have not only their professional interest to protect, but also class standards to maintain. They are members of a petty bourgeoisie, and it would seem naive to imagine that 20 hours of RAT would transform their individualistic petty bourgeois conception of the world sufficiently for them to take major initiatives against racism, when several years of sustained argument on class and sex oppression by committed political activists, has brought about no significant action from them. If RAT's claim is true, that racism is several hundred years old and is firmly embedded in people's perception, in their economic and political behaviour and in their culture and that it makes them mentally sick, then, it would surely need more concerted effort than RAT to get rid of racism.

Of course, underlying RAT claims is the assumption that social conflict can be resolved by understanding. An understanding which comes from synchronising the actual self-conception of a racist to the idea self-conception of liberal democratic ideology that the racist lives behind. By so synchronising the actual to the ideal self conception, it is thought, RAT will provide the **mechanism** for social change. No doubt this kind of synchron-isation is very desirable, but it is unlikely to bring about such change. For understanding aside, there is interest: if blacks are satisfied with Racism Awareness Training, that is what the establishment will give them. Appealing to middle-class (petty bourgeois) guilt is indeed wasted effort, since it can never lead to action. The whole basis of middle-class worthiness is that they **have** guilt feelings to agonise about. For not to feel guilty in the face of widespread oppression is callous. It is as if feeling guilty compensates us for our involvement in the capitalist system. Then, the petty bourgeoisie can busily pursue his/her individual political and economic self-interest, so long as he/she can honestly express his/her reluctant involvement with the system: it is a kind of altruistic egoism, typical of classical liberalism. Perhaps to some extent such feelings also explain the appeal of RAT to the petty bourgeoisie.

4. The Ethics of Racism Awareness Training

If it is true, that the RAT strategy is to shame and lecture people into action, and that the state **uses** RAT to manage black demands, then, both raise worrying ethical issues. But what is also morally worrying is the commercial-isation of anti-racism. The various training groups charge enormous amounts for this training. An average amount for a session (one weekend, with one trainer) is about £250. RAPU, one of the leading groups, charges a lot more than than. To quote from their handout, for a full course, they charge:

> *"£600 – plus expenses (travel, food, accommodation)...(which) cover the fees of two facilitators, preliminary planning meetings, materials etc...£25 – **Registration Fees** ...cancellation charge £75."*

Some Concluding Remarks

By this argument, it is doubtful that RAT can even achieve its modest objective to start anti-racist action and instead stands a good chance of diverting that action or even harming it. There seems no clear strategic route from this kind of consciousness-raising sessions to political action. This is not meant to imply that all anti-racist education and anti-racist consciousness training is ineffectual and harmful. Quite the contrary: both are extremely important, but need to be done in the context of concrete action. Otherwise the undoubted sincerity and energies of some of these trainers is wasted, is misused, becomes harmful and sometimes is even more unethical. It is misused because it appeals to guilt; it is wasted because it is ineffective; it is harmful because it can be appropriated by the racist state; and, it is unethical because it can also lead to the commercialisation of anti-racism. Given the absence of theoretical evaluation of RAT, it can all happen in this way – it **has** been happening in this way, relatively easily.

But these criticisms must let in no ambiguities about our intentions. Firstly, we are in no way arguing against RAT from the same point of view as racists do. We criticise RAT for not doing **enough** and for doing it badly. We criticise RAT for missed opportunities. After the 1981 rebellions, given how worried the state and its local counterparts was feeling, anti-racists who were in the position to do so, should have prized out a lot more from the establishment than a few RAT sessions. They should have also channelled their energies not in making opiate for the establishment, but in advancing the evident black unity. Secondly, it is **not** our intention to characterise **all** local state initiatives against racism as RAT sessions, or imply that all anti-racists in these institutions are pursuing the cynical ends of the establishment. There are clear examples where real mainstream anti-racist policies are backed up by political will and resources, to help end black oppression. The point is, these types of policies and action should be pursued rather than RAT.

A discussion about an alternative strategy to RAT itself deserves a separate article, but here are a few pointers:

The most sustained and the most effective initiatives against racism are already taking place in the black community. Most black communities have set up advice centres, work associations, like Asian and Afro-Caribbean workers' associations, and social clubs. There are also a number of formal and informal black political organisations such as the *Asian Youth Movement* and *Rastafarian* collectives. Thus, firstly, these black groups need to be taken very seriously. Where possible, anti-racists should support their initiatives, and get involved with their struggles, but refrain from trying to "lead" them.

Secondly, anti-racists can organise separately in existing political organisations in order to initiate policy changes and action against racism in those organisations. Where these caucus groups already exist, they should be supported in order to make effective initiatives in the mainstream of the bourgeois political process (inside and outside) the Labour Party, in women's groups, student politics and so on. The objective of such initiatives is to publicise and counter state racism. For until such oppressive legislation as the Immigration Laws, the Nationality Act, the Police Bill are removed, it is quite unlikely that there can be very effective opposition to institutionalised racism. But at the same time as these broader political measures are being pursued, caucus groups can seek to involve the mainstream of politics to also take on the daily abuses of blacks by the police force and the law courts. These groups can both support black inititiatives to set up police monitoring groups, and help expose the class and racist bias of judges.

Thirdly, anti-racist groups can be formed at work in order to directly confront institutionalised racism. Such groups can monitor recruitment, promotions and working conditions, and initiate policy objectives to change racist practices. In schools and colleges, teachers can examine the content of their curriculum and interfere with those colleagues who teach racist material. As union members we can both initiate policies and ensure that they are followed within the unions, while at the same time we mobilise the unions to confront the employer's racism. All these activities will create a lot of conflict and make anti-racists very unpopular, but much better than RAT, that would also raise **some** people's consciousness while ensuring that racists are isolated and are made ineffective.

Fourthly, as groups and as individuals, we can take on the mainstream media and set out "to win the arguments", while ensuring that the usual diet of racist humour and assumptions is consistently and relentlessly criticised. That can be done [32] by writing letters to editors and producers of newspapers and television programmes, by writing to the National Union of Journalists (NUJ) and to the NUJ Race Relations Working Group, by writing to the Press Council etc. But it is also necessary to create alternatives to the racist stereotypes by writing different material for the media, and by setting up and strengthening existing alternative radical publications.

How these things are done depends on the circumstances. On occasions black and white solidarity is useful, on other occasions separate black action is called for. The racist establishment (and some of its officers) will not like it, but if enough pressure is put on, some changes will occur in spite of their opposition. The intention is not to alienate and isolate people, but to seek support not from those who are going to divert our initiatives, but from those who are likely to maintain sustained action. Realistically, we have to assume that many will remain racist in a racist society. But blacks cannot wait until they change their minds, before they can command legitimate rights. No RAT is necessary, because the issue of racism is **not** obscure. What is needed is a political will to act and to take initiatives in our everyday affairs. In the same way as racism is not obscure, thus, effective action against racism is not new either. Most of these initiatives are already taking place, and RAT panacea can only divert us from them.

Racism awareness trainers show a great deal of optimism, enthusiasm and a lack of disabling cynicism. These are **necessary,** but not **sufficient** conditions to affect social change. For that we need sound analysis and direct empirical action in policies and conditions, and if change in thought is achieved at the same time, well and good. If not, we should be prepared to wait for it, **after** blacks receive their legitimate rights.

End Notes

1. The Department of the Environment. *Local Authorities and Racial Disadvantage:* Report of a Joint Government/Local Authority Association Working Group p33-4, 1983 HMSO.

2. ibid p34.

3. ibid.

4. ibid p35.

ibid p34-5.

6. Report of the Race Relations and Ethnic Advisor for the Borough of Haringey (Dorothy Kuya – who is also a founder member of RAPU) "Strategies for Racial Equality", p6.

7. Judy H Katz *White Awareness* University of Oklahoma Press p10 1978.

8. ibid.

9. "Racism Awarenss Training: training to make a difference" in *Community Work and Racism* ed. Ashok Ohri *et al* RKP 1982, p35.

10. Though both Manning and Ohri are presently influenced by Katz and Ivey and share many of their assumptions and strategies, their intellectual history include influences from many Third World writers. I suspect many of the trainers had a very similar history, before they were diverted by the lure of RAT.

11. Basil Manning and Ashok Ohri "Racism – the responses of community work" ed Ohri *et al* op cit p3-4

12. ibid p6.

13. ibid p11.

14. ibid p8.

15. ibid p9.

16. "White Awareness: The Frontier of Racism Awareness Training" reproduced in Ruddell D and Simpson M *Recognising Racism,* City of Birmingham Education Department p31.

17. ibid p32.

18. There is a fair amount of literature which discusses this general area. The following is a selection. Littlewood R and Lipsedge R *Aliens and Alienists: Ethnic Minorities and Psychiatry.* Penguin 1982; Holingshead A B and Redlich F C. *Social Class and Mental Illness NY, Wiley 1958; Holmes T H and Rahe R T "The Social Readjustment Rating Scale" in The Journal of Psychosomatic Research* 1967 Vol II; Thomas A and Sillen S *Racism and Psychiatry* Brunner/Manzel 1972; Szasz T *Ideology and Insanity,* Penguin 1974; Laing R D *Politics of Experience;* Rock, P. *Race, Culture and Mental* Disorder Tavistock, London 1982; Kovel J *White Racism: A Psychohistory* Vintage NY 1971.

19. Ruddell and Simpson, op cit, p32.

20. ibid, p32.

21. ibid, p30.

22. ibid, p32.

23. ibid.

24. ibid, p33.

25. A transcript of the talk, p2.

26. ibid, p4.

27. ibid, p6.

28. Ruddell and Simpson, op cit, p11.

29. Katz and Ivey passim, pp30-37.

30. Ruddell and Simpson, op cit, p28.

31. ibid, p26.

32. See Carl Gardner in 'It Ain't Half Racist Mum', Ed. P. Cohen and C. Gardner, Comedia/Carm, London 1982, pp105-110.

Appendix B

RAT and the degradation of the black struggle

By A. Sivanandan
Institute of Race Relations

RAT

There is a class war going on within Marxism as to who – in the period of the de-construction of industrial capitalism and the re-composition of the working class – are the real agents of revolutionary change: the orthodox working class, which is orthodox no more, or the 'ideological classes' who pass for the new social force or forces. It is a war that was engendered, on the one hand, by the growing disillusion with Soviet communism and, on the other, by the receding prospect of capturing state power in late capitalist societies where such power was becoming increasingly diffuse and opaque. The solution to both, on the ground, pointed to a variant of social democracy under the rubric of Eurocommunism. The solution, for theory, pointed to a re-reading of Marx, a re-hashing of Gramsci and a return to intellectual rigour accompanied by activist mortis. The working class, as a consequence, was stripped of its richest political seams – black, feminist, gay, green, etc. – and left, in the name of anti-economism, a prey to economism. Conversely, the new social forces, freed from the ballast of economic determinism (and class reductionism), have been floated as the political and ideological 'classes' of the new radicalism. But that flight from class has served only to turn ideological priorities into idealistic preoccupations, and political autonomy into personalised politics and palliatives which, for all that, have passed into common left currency and found a habitation and a name in Labour local authorities. The clearest expression of these tendencies and the mortality they bring to the new social movements are to be seen in the philosophy and practice of Racism Awareness Training (RAT), the blight of the black struggle – itself a result of the flight of race from class.

Culture, community and class

What, however, had led to the flight from class within the black community in Britain was the demise of the black community. That community – of Black, of Afro-Caribbean-Asian – had been created in the post-war years by a culture of resistance to racism in the factories and the neighbourhoods of the inner cities to which Afro-Caribbeans and Asians had been condemned to work and live. As workers, they were initially separated by a colonial division of labour which, by and large, assigned Afro-Caribbeans to the service industries and Asians to the foundries and factories. But, as denizens of the same ghetto, they found common cause against a racism that denied them their basic needs in housing, schooling and social and welfare services and brought them up against racist landlords, racist teachers, racist social workers and racist policemen. Common problems and common interests led to a common culture of resistance and to community.

That sense of community was reinforced by a common (albeit different) tradition of struggle against colonialism in Africa, Asia and the Caribbean. Nkrumah, Nehru, Garvey, Padmore, James, Williams were all stars of a common constellation, and the struggles of one continent flowed and ebbed into the struggles of the other. So that when the trade unions refused to take up the cause of the Afro-Caribbean or Asian workers over industrial disputes or racial discrimination and/or exploitation, black communities closed ranks behind them and gave them the sustenance and the support to mount a protest or conduct a strike. And that then wove the interests of the class into the concerns of the community and made for a formidable political force far in excess of its numbers.

The direction for that political force and its ideological tenets came from a variety of black marxist organisations (the Indian Workers' Association (IWA) and the Universal Coloured Peoples' Association (UCPA) foremost among them) which, in reaction to the eurocentrism of the white metropolitan left and its attempts to subsume race to class, held this much in common: that the unity and autonomy of black struggle could only enrich and politicise the struggles of the class as a whole. That did not mean that they were culturally exclusive. On the contrary, their struggles, though informed by a resistance to the oppression of black people, were directed towards the liberation of the class. And in this, they were guided by the understanding that any struggle against racism which deepened and extended the class struggle was the right struggle. Conversely, any struggle that led to the cul de sac of reactionary nationalism was the wrong one. Hence their stand: for the blacks and therefore for the class.

This politics was, in turn, fed back to the community, in the temples and the churches and Sunday schools, and through meetings and marches and news-sheets and pamphlets that linked the struggles here to the struggles back home and made common cause with the movements in Africa and Asia and the Caribbean. And it was this common and burgeoning culture of active resistance to racism and imperialism that cohered black community, linked race to class and engendered the struggles of the second generation.[1]

It was no accident, therefore, that the state should, as of nature, go for the cultural jugular of the black movement, with strategies to disaggregate that culture into its constituent parts – and then put them up for integration. And integration, as defined by Home Secretary Roy Jenkins in May 1966, was to be seen 'not as a flattening process of assimilation but as equal opportunity accompanied by cultural diversity, in an atmosphere of mutual tolerance'. But 'equal opportunity' never got off the ground, nor was meant to, and the plea for 'mutual tolerance' proved to be conclusively cynical with the passage of yet another racist Immigration Act two years later. The emphasis was on 'cultural diversity' – and the integration of those cultures into a 'cultural' pluralist set-up. Racism was not a matter of racial oppression and exploitation, of race and class, but of cultural differences and their acceptability. The 1965 White Paper had got it wrong in trying to get the National Committee for Commonwealth Immigrants (NCCI) to teach British culture to 'coloured immigrants'. But the Race Relations Act of 1968* was going to teach immigrant cultures to the white power structure instead through a national Community Relations Commission (CRS) and its myriad provincial progeny – and so minimise the social and political cost of racial exploitation. And to facilitate that process in the most fraught areas of urban deprivation, the government would provide special financial aid – some of which might even trickle down to 'the Coloured quarter'.

But that type of multiculturalism did not quite work out either. Explaining West Indian and Asian peoples to white groups and individuals in positions of power – as the CRC did or picking (ineffectually) at racial discrimination – as the Race Relations Board (RRB) was wont to do – seemed to have little effect in managing racism or breaking down black resistance. Nor had urban aid reached the parts (of society) that would have lubricated

---

*This was meant to balance out the Commonwealth Immigrants Act of a few months earlier (which denied British citizenship to British Asians in Kenya). For, as Hattersley had said, 'without integration limitation is inexcusable, without limitation integration is impossible'.

such a strategy; and, though a class of black collaborators was springing up in the shadow of the CRC and the RRB, they were still too few in number to take the heart out of black protest. And to make matters worse, the (Tory) government brought in yet another Immigration Act (1971)* stopping dead all primary immigration and putting all dependants on a hit list (those, that is, who were waiting in their countries of origin to join their families in Britain). [2]

A different struggle...

The Act may have diverted the struggles of the black community, and the Asians in particular, from the (political) fight against racism to the more legalistic fight for entry permits for their dependants. But, by creating an official category of illegal immigrants (and overstayers) and setting up a special police unit (IIIU) to pursue them, the Act served also to stoke the fires of black resistance. Already, Afro-Caribbean youth were being brutalised by the police and criminalised by the 'Sus' law; now, the Asians were suspected of being illegals and so open to arrest in their work-places or their homes. And on the streets, the sport of Paki-bashing had grown, with police indifference (if not connivance), into more generalised and organised racial violence. In education, the relegation of Afro-Caribbean children to ESN schools and the dispersal of Asian children to schools outside their neighbourhoods combined to agitate black parents. On the shopfloor, the power of the employers (heightened by the Industrial Relations Act of 1971) was compounded by the racism of the unions.

And as racism intensified, the resistance to it intensified too but in different ways from the 1950s and 1960s. Whereas the struggles of that period had been taken up with the 'first-generation' fight against brutal racism that denied basic needs and services to Afro-Caribbeans and Asians, those of the late 1960s and early 1970s had to address themselves to creating a social and educational infrastructure for the second generation – in self-help groups and social centres, supplementary schools and neighbourhood schools, workshops and bookshops, hostels for the unemployed and the homeless, youth clubs and associations. And because of the differential racism now visited on the different communities, these activities themselves became differentiated as between Afro-Caribbean and Asian. But they still found their expression in and through political groups and organisations – which, if they tended to be less 'universal' than the UCPA (1967-1971), less

*The Tory government is mentioned not because there is any difference between Tory and Labour Immigration Acts – Callaghan, the Home Secretary in the previous Labour government, had in fact foreshadowed the 1971 Act by preventing the entry of fiancés except that with every one of its Acts to restrict numbers, Labour had a balancing Act to restrict social dislocation.

generalised than the IWA (now split three ways), still came together to gather the community and mount a protest, organise a march, set up a picket. And through their newspapers and bulletins and demonstrations, they continued to connect the struggles of black people in Britain to the struggles of the Third World, the struggle against racism with the struggle against imperialism. The parameters of struggle were still the same as in the decade before except that now, with the second generation, the priorities of resistance were beginning to change. And, though there was still a culture of resistance that held black communities together and made for race/class struggle, this owed more to the self-conscious ideology of black political parties and organisations than to spontaneous local community initiatives.

Besides, the deployment of black workers itself had changed from the earlier period: they were scattered now in various industries and not necessarily concentrated (race-wise) in a few. Hence the strikes of '72, '73, '74 in the East Midlands (Nottingham, Loughborough, Leicester), Birmingham, Greater London were distinguished not only by the support they received from black political organisations, but also by their attempts to break down the racism of the trade unions and involve them more directly in black workers' struggle.* 'Unions, after all, were the organisations of their class and, however vital their struggles as blacks, to remain a people apart would be to set back the class struggle itself: the struggle against racism was still a struggle for the class.' [3]

The politics of the black youth, however, were of a different order. They were not prepared to do the 'shit work' that their (immigrant) parents had been forced to do – they wanted what they were entitled to as of right – and their politics were therefore insurrectionary. Nor were they prepared to put up with mounting police harassment and brutality – which, in 1972, had received the blessing of the press and, in 1973, the government's imprimatur.** A series of running battles with the police marked the early years of the 1970s – at Brockwell Park Fair, for instance, in 1973, and at the Carib Club (1974) and in Chapeltown, Leeds, on bonfire night (1975) – and exploded into direct confrontation with bricks and bottles and burning of police cars at the Notting Hill Carnival of 1976.

...and a different state strategy

Already, by 1974, the anxieties of the state had begun to shift from the resistances of the first generation to those of the second. The 1968 version of multiculturalism cum urban aid had clearly failed because it was aimed primarily at the white power structure. All it had done was to spawn a nursery

---

*From this emerged the first National Committee for Trade Unions Against Racialism (1973)
**The White Paper on Police-Immigrant Relations (1973) warned of 'a small minority of young coloured people...anxious to imitate behaviour amongst the black community in the United States'.

of comprador blacks – in the race relations industry. The new labour strategy of multiculturalism-with-urban-aid, therefore, would be aimed at the black communities – financing in particular the *respective* self-help projects of Asian and Afro-Caribbeans, which were starved of funds. Accordingly, in January 1975, the Home Office announced the granting of aid to 'urban areas facing special social problems' to the tune of £7,000,000, funding a host of black community groups in the process. [4] And in September of that same year, the (Labour) government indicated in a White Paper on Racial Discrimination its intention this time to include effective equal opportunities programmes into its multicultural strategy. For 'the character of the coloured population resident in this country has changed dramatically over the decade ... and the time is not far off when the majority of the coloured population will be British born' – and it was 'vital to tap the reservoirs of resilience, initiative and vigour in the racial minority groups and not to allow them to lie unused or to be deflected into negative protests on account of arbitrary and unfair discriminatory practices'. [5]

The strategy and purpose of the White Paper, and the Race Relations Act that followed from it (1976), have been anticipated and analysed in 'Race, class and the state' (1976). *For my argument here, what is important to note is that the combined strategy of promoting individual cultures, funding self-help groups and setting down anti-discriminatory and equal opportunity guidelines, not least through the collapsing of the RRB and CRC into a single Commission for Racial Equality (CRE), began finally to break down the earlier cohesion of culture, community and class. Multiculturalism deflected the political concerns of the black community into the cultural concerns of different communities, the struggle against racism to the struggle for culture. Government funding of self-help groups undermined the self-reliance, the self-created social and economic base, of those groups: they were no longer responsive to or responsible for the people they served – and service itself became a profitable concern.

Anti-discriminatory action was either ineffectual or touched only the cultural fringes of discrimination so that you could wear a turban and still get a job – and behind equal opportunity, based as it was on the concept of racial disadvantage (as opposed to institutional racism), hovered the notion of differential opportunities for Asians and West Indians

---

*'Within ten years Britain will have solved its "black problem" – but "solved" in the sense of having diverted revolutionary aspiration into nationalist achievement, reduced militancy to rhetoric, put protest to profit and, above all, kept a black underclass from bringing to the struggles of the white workers political dimensions peculiar to its own historic battle against capital.' [6]

respectively. [7] If opportunity there was, it was opportunity for the 'black' compradors, preened and pruned by the CRE to blossom into the new 'black' leadership, and later the 'state-class', that would manage racism and keep the lid on protest – or at least deflect it from political struggle. And as a further bonus, Labour had, under the previous Tory administration, been gifted a cross-section of Asian business men from Uganda (passing for refugees), presumably to add to 'the leaven of energy and resourcefulness that immigrant communities brought with them'. [8]

Underlying the whole of the state's project was a divisive culturalism that turned the living, dynamic, progressive aspects of black people's culture into artefact and habit and custom – and began to break up community.

In fact, the collapse of the long-standing strike at Grunwick at the end of 1977 owes not a little to this process. The strikers (predominantly Asian women in a predominantly Asian workforce) , it has been argued by some black activists, would have done better to have relied on the black community and black organisations for their support than to have looked to the trade unions – who finally betrayed them. [9] But except for the support of women and of the odd black organisation, that community, which as recently as 1973-74 had rallied to a series of black strikes in the East Midlands, was no longer there. And even in the strikes that followed Grunwick's in the next couple of years – as at Futters, and Chix – it was the women in the black community who turned out to help the class.

Black women had 'held up half the sky', without getting half the recognition, during the black power era. But now, when the rest of the community was falling away, it was they who stood out against the skyline. And, informed not only by their struggles against racism and sexism but by those of their sisters against sexism and imperialism in the Third World, it was they who found common cause with the class.*

It was the women, besides, who had to bear the brunt of the cuts in health, education and welfare which marked the last years of Callaghan's Labour government. These affected Asian and Afro-Caribbean families in particular, and it was the women from the communities who took up the issues of child care (Afro-Caribbean and Asian), black prisoners' rights (Afro-Caribbean), the virginity testing and X-raying of immigrants (Asian), the enforced use of depo-provera (Afro-Caribbean and Asian), the neglect of 'ethnic diseases' such as sickle cell anaemia (Afro-Caribbean) and rickets (Asian),

---

*By 1978, black women's groups had sprung up all over Britain and came together to form one powerful national body, the Organisation of Women of Asian and African Descent (OWAAD), with a national newspaper, FOWAAD. [10]

the easy relegation of Afro-Caribbean children to adjustment units ('sin-bins') and the fight against the deportation of 'illegal' (Asian) mothers or for the entry of 'illegal' (Asian) children to join them. But, of their very nature, these issues had a differential impact on the two communities and tended to make for separate struggles on the ground. And although ideologically the black women's movement still tried to cohere the common interests of race, gender and class, the black culture of resistance of an earlier period was now being put under review by a feminist culture of resistance which was still not confident enough to create new black parameters.

From black struggle to anti-racist struggle

The struggles of the youth, already divided by the propagation of multi-culture, had also taken off in different directions. The trouncing the police had received at the hands of the Afro-Caribbean youth at the Notting Hill Carnival (1976) had only led to a more sophisticated, mailed-fist velvet-glove, approach to policing. The tactic of using the media to legitimate the criminalisation of black youth, first begun under Police Commissioner Robert Mark, was continued by his successor, David McNee – only he, taking to heart his nickname 'The Hammer', now brought riot shields to the 'defence' of his force. And increasing police authoritarianism itself found legitimacy in the policies of a Labour government which, with an eye to the forthcoming elections, had begun to back-pedal on its anti-discriminatory programme (however ineffective) and rely instead on the forces of law and order to smother black discontent.

Labour had earlier – as part of its balancing act between restricting immigration and improving integration – started yet another Dutch auction on immigration control through, this time, a Green Paper on Nationality Law. The Tories, under Thatcher, upped the ante and promised pass laws to control 'internal immigration' and 'arrangements' to facilitate voluntary repatriation. And the National Front, thus released into respectability, became more brazen in its attacks on the Asian community – and so occupied the attention of Asian youth. But since the Front's bravery was invariably under 'police protection', the Asian youth were up against the police as well. The killing of Gurdip Singh Chaggar in 1976 by young fascist thugs in the heart of Southall had led to clashes with the police (who held that the murder was not necessarily racial). In 1977, the Front, under police escort, had staged virulently racist and provocative marches through black city areas and were stopped by the youth of both communities. In 1978, Judge McKinnon ruled that the National Party leader Kingsley Read's pronouncement on Chaggar's murder – 'one down, one million to go' – did not constitute incitement to racial hatred.* In 1979, the Front, abetted by the policies of the local Tory council and the police, flaunted its fascist election programmes in Southall Town Hall and was repelled by the citizenry, but at the cost of the life of a teacher, who was battered to death by the Special Patrol Group.

The rise of the right had, three years earlier, brought together radical whites and blacks in the inner-city areas in an Anti-Racist Anti-Fascist Co-ordinating Committee (ARAFCC) with its own newspaper, CARF. Their battle was joined a year later by white organisations under the broad banner of the Anti-Nazi League (ANL). But, in the process, the direction of the battle got deflected from a fight against racism and, therefore, fascism, to a fight against fascism and, incidentally, racism. The whites from the local committees of ARAFCC defected to the ANL, which, with its spectacular events such as rock concerts and fetes and carnivals, its youth organisations such as School Kids Against the Nazis and its paper SKAN, and its mass leafleting drives, was able to attract more (white) support and mobilise more (white) people. The fascists, as a result, were stopped dead in their electoral tracks; but they were also driven from the (white) high streets into the (black) alley ways of the inner city, there to continué their depredations and their recruitment. And when, after the general election of 1979, the ANL (its mission accomplished) disbanded, the issues of racism and fascism had become separated, and the joint struggles of Asians and Afro-Caribbeans likewise. The black struggle (for community and class) was becoming more narrowly a struggle against racism, and the anti-racist struggle itself was tending to divide into struggles that concerned Asians (mainly) and the struggles that concerned Afro-Caribbeans (mainly).** The protest over Akhtar Ali Baig's murder (July 1980) in Newham, for example, was mostly an Asian affair, and the massive march following the burning to death of thirteen young Afro-Caribbeans in a fire in New Cross (January 1981) chiefly an Afro-Caribbean one.

And then, in the summer of 1981, the youth of the benighted inner cities, black and white, Afro-Caribbean and Asian, came together again not so much in joint struggle as in a blinding moment of spontaneous insurrection against the impossibility of their common condition. For, in the course of two brief years, Thatcherite monetarism had blighted the future of all working-class youth, not just black, and left them a bleak landscape of 'rocks, moss, stonecrop, iron, merds' over-shadowed by policemen.

---

*'In this England of ours', the good judge observed, 'we are allowed to have our own view still, thank goodness, and long may it last.'
** But not before the Indian Workers' Association, the Black Socialist Alliance, Blacks Against State Harassment and various black women's groups had organised one final national demonstration against state harassment and fascist thuggery – in June 1979.

The rebellions shook the government. The danger now was not the black community as such. There was no black community. The promotion of cultural separatism (euphemistically known as cultural diversity or multiculturalism) was keeping Asians and Afro-Caribbeans apart; the development of a youth culture and a women's culture were further de-composing the forces within the community, without, as yet, realigning them in a new black configuration; and the emergence of an Afro-Caribbean managerial class in the race relations industry (and sub-managers in the nationalised self-help groups), together with the flowering of Ugandan-Asian entrepreneurship, were breaking up community into classes. The danger to the state stemmed from the never-employed youth of the inner cities, both black and white, hounded and harried by the police. But the blacks, by virtue of their racial oppression, were the insurrectionary tinder.*

Hence, while a Task Force of town planners and bankers and business-men under the Minister for the Environment was sent to study mixed areas like Toxteth in Liverpool, to see how such areas could be regenerated, black (mainly Afro-Caribbean) areas like Brixton got the attention also of a quasi-judicial inquiry under Lord Scarman to investigate the 'disorders' and their causes (in racism and police-black relations). Little of substance came out of the first of these initiatives for Toxteth (or Smethwick) as such, but the Urban Aid Programme, which under the Tories, had fallen into disfavour, now received a 'dramatic re-awakening of interest...as a vehicle for social measures in multi-racial areas', and the CRE, which the Tories had threatened to close down, was open to business again – the business of channelling funds to black 'self-help' groups.** Consequently, 'funding for the total urban programme ... was dramatically increased, against the trend, to a 1982/3 level of £270m.'***

The rise and rise of ethnicity

It was Lord Scarman's report, however, that pointed to a new ethnic strategy,

---

* 'To allege that unemployment or social deprivation is the cause of the "riots" is to pretend that racism is not also the cause of unemployment and social deprivation – among blacks.' [11]

** Though Section 11 of the Local Government Act of 1966 is the 'major vehicle of...government support for local authority programmes designed to combat racial disadvantage', 'the Urban Programme is the major source of funding for voluntary sector schemes designed to combat racial discrimination...' [12]

*** 'Nationally, over 200 new "ethnic projects" have been approved for 1982/3; in the Partnership authorities these are valued at £2m (£0.77m in 1981/2) while traditional Urban Programme expenditure on "ethnic projects" has increased still more sharply to £7m (£2.7m in 1981/2). It is estimated that £15m is currently being spent on ethnic projects under the urban programme.' [13]

which was received with enthusiasm (and relief) by Tory and Labour alike.* The foundation for that strategy, however, had already been intimated in the report of the Home Affairs Committee on Racial Disadvantage (1981) – which was itself informed by a whole school of ethnicity that had emerged (at Bristol University's Social Science Research Council Unit on Ethnic Relations) to take on the 'problem' of British-born blacks.**

Whereas multiculturalism, addressing itself to the revolt of the first-generation 'immigrant', diagnosed the problem as one of cultural misunderstanding, the ethnicists, in trying to relate to the ongoing revolt of British-born blacks, connected it with the cultural limbo to which racism had ostensibly condemned them. Neither Asian/Afro-Caribbean nor British but afflicted by both, the second generation was adrift of its moorings and rudderless, caught in a cross-current of emotion in its search for identity – not least, to fight racism with. And in that search, it kept returning to its ethnicity and, redefining it, found refuge therein. Ethnicity refers, therefore, to the creation of a new reactive culture on the part of British-born Asians and West Indians alike. But where Asians tended to go into their cultures to make the new ethnicity, West Indian ethnicity came out of a mixture, a 'creolisation', of Afro-Caribbean culture with the 'host' culture. 'Those who were born in Britain', states Watson, 'are caught between the cultural expectations of their parents (the first-generation migrants) and the social demands of the wider society. Young Sikhs and Jamaicans, for instance, often feel that they do not "fit" in either culture ... Largely in response to racism, these two minorities have begun a process of ethnic redefinition – or "creolisation" ...
[15] Or, in Weinreich's language: 'West Indian boys have conflicted identifications with the general representatives of their own ethnicity and the native white population.' Hence, the 'changes' in the second generation should be seen as 'redefinition of their ethnic distinctiveness'. [16] It is racism, however, according to the Ballards, that has 'precipitated a reactive pride in their separate ethnic identity'. [17] Ethnicity itself, for Wallman, is a 'perception' of difference, a 'sense' of it, something that was 'felt" a clue to identity. [18]

By acknowledging the resistance to racism on the part of the second generation only to banish it to 'conflicted identification' and 'ethnic redefinition', the ethnicists deny the connection between race and class

---

But then, it was in essence an elaboration of the multicultural strategy initiated by Labour in 1976 – and in hard times, the Tories were not averse to taking lessons from their masters in social control.

**Ethnicity, which became muted when the Unit moved to Aston University under Professor John Rex in 1979, [14] is soon to be revived by Professor Robin Cohen (with Rex) in a five-year (policy-oriented) research programme at Warwick University.*

and between racism and imperialism and reincarcerate the second generation in the castle of their skin. Identity is all. The Home Affairs Committee then takes on the ethnic theme and, making ethnicity official, signs up institutional racism as racial disadvantage – leaving it to Scarman to tie it up with ethnic need.

Like the Race Relations Act of 1976, the main planks of the Scarman report were racial discrimination (direct and indirect) and racial disadvantage. Racial discrimination Scarman, too, was prepared to leave the 'existing law' and presumably the CRE.* But racial disadvantage , which the 1976 Act – steering its way between the Scylla of institutional racism and Charybdis of inherent inferiority had left (undefined) to the vagaries of Equal Opportunity, was in Scarman to be (specifically) treated in terms of special ethnic needs and problems.** And it is here at the point of cure, in the act of applying the ethnic poultice to the ethnic wound, that racial disadvantage begins to smell of inherent disability.

The West Indian family, implies Scarman, is comparatively unstable, 'doubtless because of the impact of British social conditions on the matriarchal extended family structure of the West Indian immigrants'. [19] For instance, 'the percentage of children in care and of single-parent families in the black community is noticeably higher than one would expect in relation to the proportion of black people in the community as a whole. Fifty percent of single parent families in ... Lambeth in 1978 were non-white'. Besides, 'the two areas where the April disorders were centred – Tulse Hill and Herne Hill – contain some 22 percent of all single parent households in Lambeth and 2.1 percent of the 0-18 group in those wards are in care. Of the 185 children in care of those two wards on 10 September 1980, 112 (61%) were black'. In addition, it was estimated that '200-300 young blacks are homeless, sleeping rough or squatting in Brixton'.

Young West Indians, for Scarman are 'a people of the street ... They live their lives on the street, having nothing better to do: they make their protest there: and some of them live off street crime.' Inevitably, they must come into contact with the police, 'whom they see as pursuing and harassing them on the streets'.*** And this hostility of the black youth to the police has '*infected* older members of the community' (emphasis added). The street-corners are 'social centres' for the old people too, and 'young and old, good and bad have time on their hands and a continuing opportunity ... to engage

---

The CRE was under inquiry by the Home Affairs Committee at the time and Scarman would not commit himself.

**'The special problems and needs of the ethnic minorities', is how Scarman put it.*

***By contrast, the 'chief complaint of Asian leaders appears to be that the police do not do sufficient to protect their community from alleged attacks by racist members of the white community.' [20]*

in endless discussion of their grievances', so that 'in Brixton even one isolated instance of misconduct can foster a whole legion of rumours which rapidly become beliefs held within the community'.

If this is not as elaborate as Moynihan's 'tangled pathology' of the American 'Negro family',* it is because Scarman's brief was to investigate the 'Brixton disorders' not the West Indian community. But, given his determination to acquit the state of institutional racism, it was inevitable that he should find the West Indian community guilty of inherent disability and so give racial disadvantage a meaning which even the Home Affairs Committee report on the subject (July 1981) had been careful to avoid. But the committee, since its brief was racial disadvantage as such, also referred to the disadvantage suffered by the Asian community and located it in language, religion, custom and (peasant) illiteracy. (Only the 'East African Asians' were an exception.) Between them, the two reports set out the terms of the West Indian and Asian ethnic need and provided the criteria on which the government based its (ethnic) programmes and allocated its (ethnic) funds.

The ensuing scramble for government favours and government grants (channelled through local authorities) on the basis of specific ethnic needs and problems served, on the one hand, to deepen ethnic differences and foster ethnic rivalry and, on the other, to widen the definition of ethnicity to include a variety of national and religious groups – Chinese, Cypriots, Greeks, Turks, Irish, Italians, Jews, Muslims, Sikhs – till the term itself became meaningless (except as a means of getting funds). This 'vertical mosaic' of ethnic groups, so distanced from the horizontal of class politics, then became even more removed by the policies of 'left' Labour councils who, lacking the race-class perspective which would have allowed them to dismantle the institutional racism of their own structures, institutionalised ethnicity instead. And it was left to a handful of genuinely anti-racist programmes and/or campaigns, such as those against deportation, police harassment and racial violence (sustained largely by GLC funding), to carry on the dwindling battle for community and class.

The other cure for racial disadvantaged propounded by Scarman was 'positive action', which meant no more than a determined effort at promoting equal opportunity, or, more precisely, reducing unequal opportunity for ethnic minorities, but backed up this time by a system of monitoring. And this, too, was taken up avidly by inner-city administrations who, having set up their own race relations units (to administer ethnic programmes and ethnic funds), required now an ethnic staff not least, to keep an eye on jobs

---

'Once or twice removed, it (the weakness of the family structure) will be found to be the principal source of most of the aberrent, inadequate or anti-social behaviour that did not establish, but now serves to perpetuate the cycle of poverty and deprivation. [21]

for ethnics.*

Underlying the whole of Scarman's report is a socio-pychological view of racism, resonant of the ideas of the ethnic school, which, when coupled with his views on racial disadvantage, verges on the socio-biological. Institutional racism, for Scarman, is not a reality of black life but a matter of subjective feelings, perceptions, attitudes, beliefs. Ethnic minorities have a 'sense' of 'concealed discrimination'. Young blacks have a 'sense of rejection' and 'a sense of insecurity'. They do not 'feel' secure socially, economically or politically. They 'see' policemen 'as pursuing and harassing them on the streets' – and the older generation have come to share this 'belief'. (The 'belief' in the Asian community is that the police do not protect them against the 'alleged' racist attacks.) Community 'attitudes and beliefs' (caused by a lack of confidence in the police) underlay the disturbances. 'Popular atitudes and beliefs' themselves 'derive their strength' from the 'limbo of the half remembered and the half-imagined'. The 'image' of a hostile police force is 'myth' and 'legend'. [22]

Equally, if the police force were guilty of anything, it was not institutional racism but racial prejudice – which 'does manifest itself occasionally in the behaviour of a few police officers on the street.' And the breakdown of police-community relations was, on the part of the police, due to the fact that their 'attitudes and methods' had not quite caught up with 'the problem of policing a multicultural society'. Part of the policeman's training, therefore, should be directed to 'an understanding of the cultural backgrounds and attitudes of ethnic minorities.'

Racism, for Scarman, was in the mind – in attitudes, prejudices, irrational beliefs – and these were to be found on both sides of the divide – black and white. Institutional racism was a matter of black perception, white racism was a matter of prejudice. Or that, on the face of it, was what Scarman seemed to be saying – and at worst, it was even-handed, liberal even. But what he had effectively done was to reduce institutional racism to black perception and replace it with personal prejudice – and so shift the object of anti-racist struggle from the state to the individual, from changing society to changing people, from improving the lot of whole black communities, mired in racism and poverty, to improving the lot of 'black' individuals.

It was a plan that the nascent 'black' petit-bourgeoisie, nourished on government (and local government) aid for ethnic need and positive action for ethnic equality leapt to embrace. By and large, the ethnics were content to fight each other in their quest for office. And it was only when there was a white blockage in the system, preventing them from going up further, that

*The local CRC's were pushed on the sidelines in the process and the central CRE was left the statutory task of taking up cases of discrimination.

the ethnics turned 'black' and pulled out all their oppressed 'black' history to beat the whites with. Hence the demand for Black Sections in the Labour Party; the rise and fall of the Black Media Workers' Association (BMWA) (the fall coming after the white media made room for them in ethnic slots since when, they have gone back to being Afro-Caribbeans or Asians respectively); and the emergence of the black trade union aristocracy, the Black Trade Union Solidarity Movement (BTUSM).* None of these give a fart for ordinary black people, but use them and their struggles as cynically as any other bourgeois class or sub-class.

Ironically enough, most of the support for these groups has come from the 'left-wing' of the Labour Movement which, having failed to incorporate black working-class struggles and black working-class leadership into its own history and organisation, now feels compelled to accommodate black sects in its vaunted broad church. Taking black out of the context of the struggles in which it was beaten into a political colour, the white left now believes that any self-seeking middle-class group that calls itself black has an automatic right to appropriate that history and is automatically political or progressive. What is even more ironical is that this should be happening at a time when, in the rush for office, even such reconstituted blackness is breaking up into Afro-Caribbean and Asian, with the Afro-Caribbeans claiming a prior right to black history on the basis, simply, of a darker colour – thereby emptying 'black' of politics altogether.** Black Sections are no more representative of black working people than the Labour Party is of white. In fact, black politics has to cease to be political for blacks to get into politics. The BTUSM is no more interested in the lot of the rank and file than their lordships Chapple and Murray were as erstwhile leaders of their unions. The BMWA, in the short period of its fight-to-get-into-Channel-4 existence, never did anything for the lower ranks of black workers or, for that matter, demanded to make political black plays or programmes that would have improved the lot of ordinary Afro-Caribbeans or Asians unless exposing the foibles and manners of one's own people to white voyeurs, but from the inside this time, can be considered funny or political. But then, an ethnic media can only reproduce the cult of ethnicity. And a culture of ethnicity, unlike a culture of resistance has no community and has no class.

And to undergird it all, undergird the efforts of the new ethnics to move up and away – up through the white blockages in the system and

---

* *The personnel of one group were frequently the personnel of another, as in an interlocking directorate.*
**This degradation of 'black' has now passed into vulgar usage and separated Afro-Caribbeans from Asians – as in 'black and Asian', which is itself a nonsense, as one refers to colour (not politics) and the other to geography.*

away from the black communities and their troubles – there is a whole school of thought and enterprise which promises to change white minds and white attitudes so that a thousand black flowers can blossom in the interstices of the white structure. Felicitously, it calls itself RAT (Racism Awareness Training)* and it is to this final degradation of black struggle that I now turn my attention.

The birth of RAT

RAT began life in HAT (Human Awareness Training) on a military base in Florida at the end of the 1960s, when the reverberations of black rebellion in American cities began to resonate in the military installations in the US and Japan and drove the Defense Department to a Human Goals Proclamation upholding individual dignity, worth and equal opportunity in its ranks. The training of human relations instructors at the Defense Race Relations Institute (DRRI), therefore, was meant to inculcate a knowledge of minority cultures and history, together with an understanding of personal racism.

HAT, of course, had formed part of human relations training for some time, but the race relations element came into prominence only after the Kerner Commission (1968) declared that racism in America was a white problem and that it inhered in the very structures of society. 'What white Americans have never fully understood – but what the Negro can never forget – is that white society is deeply implicated in the ghetto. White institutions created it, white institutions maintain it and white society condones it. [23] On the face of it, the Kerner report looked like a radical statement (as radical as Scarman appeared liberal), and though it connected racism with white institutions, nowhere did it connect the institutions themselves with an exploitative white power structure. So that oppression was severed from exploitation, racism from class and institutional racism from state racism.

The US Commission on Civil Rights (1970) echoed the Kerner Commission and went on to define racism (which Kerner had left undefined) as 'any attitude, action or institutional structure which subordinates a person or group because of his or their color', adding that an 'institutional structure was any well-established, habitual or widely accepted pattern of action' (i.e., behavioural) or 'organizational arrangements whether formal or informal' (i.e., administrational). The Commission also made a distinction between 'overt racism' and 'indirect institutional subordination' (which was to become direct and indirect discrimination in the British context). And combating racism, stated the Commission, involved 'changing the

---

* *Some RAT practitioners have recently changed the name to TIRA (Training in Racism Awareness); but a RAT by any other name still smells.*

behaviour of whites' and 'increasing the capabilities of non-white groups' (which in Britain was to become known as tackling racial disadvantage). But the principal responsibility was 'with the white community rather than within the non-white communities'. [24]

Following the two reports, a whole host of literature sprang up in education, psychology and the churches, rescuing racism from structural taint and interiorising it within the white psyche and white behaviour and formulating programmes for combating racism on that basis. The New York-based Council for Interracial Books, Integrated Education (Chicago), the Foundation for Change and the Detroit-centred New Perspectives on Race were particularly active in the educational field. Writing in *Integrated Education,* Paul Goldin formulated a 'Model for racial awareness training of teachers in integrated schools' which 'pushes one (through inter-racial confrontation) into an identification with the minority position'. [25] In *Developing New Perspectives on Race,* however, Michigan's school superintendent, Patricia Bidol, advocated a more cognitive approach, emphasising that 'only whites can be racists because it is whites that have control over the institutions that create and enforce American cultural norms and values' – and it is whites who benefit from it. She distinguished, therefore, between overt (Archie Bunker type) racism and covert (unintentional) racism and defined racism itself as 'prejudice plus institutional power'. And it was Bidol and Detroit's New Perspectives on Race who pioneered in the development of racism awareness training for educators.* [26]

But the work of the Detroit Industrial Mission – following the burning of the city (1967) and the rise of black militancy in DRUM (Dodge Revolutionary Union Movement) – and FRUM (Ford Revolutionary Union Movement) pointed to the need to create a 'new white consciousness' through both attitudinal and behavioural change. The emphasis hitherto, wrote its Associate Director Robert W. Terry in *For whites only,* had been on changing attitudes to change behaviour or changing behaviour (through law, for instance) in order to change attitudes. But though both attitudes and behaviour were critical and both needed to be changed, "attitudes will be misplaced and behaviour misdirected if consciousness remains untouched'.

For even the most well-intentioned person, argues Terry, taking on from

---

* *Bidol's influence is also prominent in Britain, as for instance in the use of her slide show, 'From racism to pluralism', at RAT sessions run by the Racism Awareness Programme Unit (RAPU).*

where the Civil Rights Commission had left off,* without being 'personally involved in overt acts of racial injustice', can perpetuate racism in institutions merely by the way the American 'cultural or belief system... sets his orientation in the decision-making process'. Hence, it was important to be conscious of cultural (historical, linguistic, etc.) institutional (direct and indirect) and individual racism all at once. [28] Cultural racism had to be examined wherever it occurred (language, textbooks, media), 'confrontation' was a good way of challenging personal racism and, for institutional racism, Terry provided a model check list designed by the Chicago Campaign for One Society: 'Inventory of racism: how to look for institutional racism'.**

The elements of the RAT credo were already set by the time Judy Katz came to write her D.Ed thesis: *Systematic handbook of exercises for the re-education of white people with respect to attitudes and behaviourisms* (1976) – except that by now she could also draw on the Women's Movement for an even more personal interpretation of oppression and the need for consciousness-raising. That perspective would, in addition, also allow her (and her followers) to distort the language, style and analysis of the black movement and further remove racism from its exploitative context and render it class-less.

Racism, states Katz, is indeed a white problem, and white people had better take conscience of it – for the sake of their own mental health. As far back as 1965, she points out, the Commission on Mental Health described racism as the number one mental health problem in the United States. 'Its destructive effects severely cripple the growth and development of millions of our citizens, young and old alike.' [29] Even before that, the Myrdal 'report' on 'The American Dilemma' (1944) had drawn attention to the hiatus, the schism, the rupture in the (white) American psyche: between 'American ideals of equality, freedom, God-given dignity of the individual, inalienable rights' and 'the practices of discrimination, humiliation, insult, denial of opportunity to Negroes and others in a racist society'. [30] New research had sprung up to show that racism was a 'psychological problem... deeply imbedded in white people from a very early age both on a conscious and an unconscious level'. And even black commentators, according to Katz, confirmed the diagnosis, pointed to a cure – like Whitney Young, for instance, head of the National Urban League: '...most people are not conscious of what racism really is. Racism is not a desire to wake up every morning and lynch a black man from a tall tree. It is not engaging in vulgar epithets...It is the day to day indignities, the subtle humiliations that are so devastating...The Kerner Commission has said that if you have been an

---

* 'Even many whites who sincerely abhor racism in principle and openly combat overt racism, sometimes feel themselves resisting clearly anti-racist actions for "intuitive" reasons they do not fully understand. This usually means such anti-racist actions threaten to reduce certain almost sub-consciously perceived psychological benefits these whites have been gaining from living in a society where they are considered members of a "superior" group.' [27]

**This same checklist is reproduced in Katz's handbook.

observer; if you have stood by idly, you are racist.'

Katz even rallies radical blacks like Du Bois to her cause: 'Am I, in my blackness, the sole sufferer? I suffer. And yet, somehow, above the suffering, above the shackled anger that beats the bars, above the hurt that crazes, there surges in me a vast pity – pity for a people imprisoned and enthralled, hampered and made miserable for such a cause.' And more recent black militants, like Stokely Carmichael, taken out of the context of struggle: 'if the white man wants to help, he can go home and free his own people', [31] or Malcolm X: 'whites who are sincere should organize themselves and figure out some strategies to break down race prejudice that exists in white communities'. *[32]

Racism, for Katz, is an 'essence' that history has deposited in the white psyche, like sexism is an 'essence' deposited in the male: oppressors oppress themselves.** It is a part of the psycho-social history of white America, part of its collective unconscious. It is in American customs, institutions, language, mores – it is both conscious and unconscious at the same time, both overt and covert. There is no escaping it. And because the system is loaded in their favour, all that whites can be, even when they fight racism, is anti-racist racists: if they don't, they are just plain, common or garden racists.

Hence, any training programme that intends to bring individual whites to a consciousness of themselves should also take conscience of American culture and institutions. And it should be done at two levels at once – the cognitive or informative and the affective or emotional at the level of thinking and at the level of feeling. The techniques that had hitherto been used in human relations training erred on one side or the other; or, like multicultural or ethnic studies, they were too other-oriented, not self-aware enough; or they were, like inter-racial encounters, too exploitative, once again, of Third World peoples. Only white on white techniques promised any success, and it was on that basis that Ms Katz had devised a systematic training programme which was influenced as much by the shift in psychotherapy towards a teaching role as the shift in education towards a counselling role.*** The point, after all, was not to change attitudes, but to change behaviour – to change the world.

Since then (1976), the Katz technique of racism awareness training, an intensive six-stage programme of forty-eight exercises crammed into two weekends but adaptable 'to many different settings', has become widely used in the United States, 'in school systems, with

---

* *RAT practitioners in Britain even quote Stokely on institutional racism.*
** *'Our sexual and racial essences have an enormous influence on our perspectives and experiences.'*
*** *Which is why her trainers carry the exotically hybrid name of 'facilitators'.*

teachers, counsellors, and administrators, as part of Affirmative Action Programmes with managers: at university communities with students, faculties, and administrators...' [3][3]

Part of its appeal lay, of course, with the American penchant for therapy, but part of it was also due to the political climate in which it grew: the collapse of the Black Power movement into culturalism and theological liberation, the personalisation of power in the Women's Movement and the diaspora of guilt broadcast by Israel in the wake of its imperial adventures.

Taking a leaf out of the Black Power book, Ms Katz defines racism as a 'white problem'. But whereas the white problem in Black Power ideology referred to the white capitalist power structure, in Ms Katz it is reduced to a personal one, a problem of individuals who, because they are white, have power – over non-whites. Having so established white guilt as irreversible, almost inborn, Ms Katz takes infinite pains to warn whites that they should not feel guilty, for guilt is 'a self indulgent way to use up energy'.* On the other hand, whites suffer from racism – as much as men suffer from sexism. And 'we have learnt from the Feminist Movement that men as well as women are adversely affected by oppressive sex roles'. Her programme of anti-racist sensitivity training, therefore, promises through a 'process of self-examination, change and action that we will someday liberate ourselves and our society'.

It is the sort of psychospiritual mumbo-jumbo which, because it has the resonances of the political movements of its time – capitalists have changed the world, our business is to interpret it – and, by reducing social problems to individual solutions, passes off personal satisfaction for political liberation, and then wraps it all up in a Madison Avenue sales package promising instant cure for hereditary disease, claimed the attention not just of Middle America but of a grateful state. For what better way could the state find to smooth out its social discordances while it carried on, untrammelled, with its capitalist works?

The spread of RAT

It was not, on the face of it, a package that would have appealed to the British 'character', but it seemed the logical extension to the work of a group of teachers and community workers (mostly black) whose campaign against racial symbols in children's books had derived its message and

---

* In one of the exercises in the Handbook, Ms Katz advises the 'facilitator' that 'one way to manage feelings of guilt is to emphasise that racism is deeply ingrained in our system and that we are clearly products of our system' – and then proceeds illogically to demand that one changes oneself rather than the system.

method directly from the Council for Interracial Books in the US who were themselves proponents of RAT. Accordingly, in 1978, the group founded the Racism Awareness Programme Unit (RAPU) on the rock of Katzian teaching and was joined soon after by renegades (mostly black) from the multicultural faith, disaffected by its inability to speak to white racism. In the following year, some of the RAPU people, along with others, set up the National Committee on Racism in Children's Books and began to produce a quarterly magazine, *Dragon's Teeth*. The journal's aim of investigating (and challenging) racial bias in children's books, however, was centred around black images and stereotypes. And this, over the next two years, led to a preoccupation with black identity and reclaiming the past —and found its obverse in white identity and RAT.

RAT, by now, had begun to make inroads into the public sector. Some interest in human relations training (including race relations) had been evinced in official circles with the rise of black youth militancy in the mid-1970s. But these, where they did obtain – principally in education, police and probation services – took the form of the occasional conference or seminar or lecture. Industry paid a little more attention to race relations, but strictly for O and M purposes, and was therefore limited, as in the work of the Industrial Language Training Centres (ILTC), to things like difficulties in communication between employers and employees because of language and culture.

By 1980, Nadine Peppard, who as Race Relations Adviser at the Home Office was responsible for developing race relations training, and advising the police, prison and probation services, was arguing for the type of affective techniques that had been developed in the US – at the DRRI in Florida, among others, and by the Council for Interracial Books. Although a more conscious effort, she felt, had recently been made in the 'practitioner services' to include 'the general question of attitudes and the psychology of prejudice', group work techniques, such as role-playing and training games, were still restricted to the industrial field (in the work of the ILTCs, for instance). 'A practical analysis of what is required', urged Ms Peppard, 'clearly shows that those attitudes or beliefs which underlie actual behaviour must be seen as the heart of the matter and that to construct a training scheme which tries to ignore them is to beg the question.' [34] An essential aspect of group work, she suggested, was the type of 'sensitivity training', 'consciousness-raising' or 'awareness training' that was 'a standard aspect of training' in the US. As a reference point and guide, she cited the 'experimental training programme' mounted at the University of Oklahoma by Professor Judy Katz.

In education too, the end of the 1970s saw a general shift of emphasis, often within multicultural teaching itself, from imparting information to challenging attitudes. Before students could understand other people's customs, they would, it appeared, have to be opened up to such understanding, made receptive to it, emotionally and mentally. Hence, a psychological or affective approach was necessary for the 'affective component "leads" to cognitive in attitude change'. [35] Information, in other words, did not change people's attitudes and behaviour. On the other hand, if you changed people's attitudes and behaviour, they would be more receptive to the information. The sociological approach of multiculturalism was yielding to the psychological approach of racism awareness training.

But not till after the riots of 1981 and Scarman did either the official race relations courses or RAPU take off seriously into RAT. For one thing, Scarman had changed the terms of debate from the material effects of racism on poor blacks to the cultural effects on and the job prospects of middle-class ethnics. For another, he had, in his recommendations on local authority spending and police training, provided a breeding-ground for RAT and the reproduction of 'imagined communities' [36] and their ethno-psychological struggles for identity against ethno-centrism.*

A flurry of reports, working groups and conferences in local authority strategies to combat racial disadvantage ensued. [37] The Minister of State for Home Affairs, declaring that 'it cannot be unfair to give help to those with a special handicap', [38] pledged central government support for local authority endeavours. Race relations subcommittees, ethnic advisers, RAT courses – and even (elected) black councillors – began to spring up – in every inner-city borough in London and the conurbations. The GLC, Brent, Haringey, Hackney, Camden, Islington, Lambeth, Newham, Northants, Coventry, Bradford, Nottingham, Leicester, Sheffield, Birmingham, Greater Manchester, Liverpool – they all had their ethnic units and ethnic officers and ethnic projects, their ethnic monitoring units and, above all, as an investment in an ethnic future, their RAT courses, some of them even compulsory for local authority staff, some of them with their own RAT inspectorate, (They were also, not fortuitously, the areas that had 'rioted' or were ripe for 'riot' in 1981.)

And yet, in terms of the material conditions of the workless, homeless, school-less, welfare-less blacks of slum city, all this paroxysm of activity has not made the blindest bit of difference. The GLC Housing Committee Chairman admitted in 1984 that racial harassment on some East London estates was 'on a scale not seen in this country for 40 to 50 years'. [39] In the same year, the Policy Studies Institute survey concluded: 'the quality of the housing of black people is much worse than the quality of housing in general

---

* *Identity is the personalisation of nationalism, ethnicity its group expression – all points in the same continuum.*

in this country.' [40] And unemployment for blacks, already twice the average for whites at the end of 1982, has worsened considerably.

All that has happened is that the centre of gravity of the race relations industry has moved from the central government and the CRE to the local state and with it, the black struggle, not for community and class any more, but for hand-outs and position.* And racism awareness, not black power, was the new ideology.

The same tendencies to ethnicising and RATifying racism were observable in education. In 1981, the Rampton Committee of Inquiry into the Education of Children from Ethnic Minority Groups, though acknowledging racism in the teaching profession, identified racism with 'a set of attitudes and behaviour towards people of another race which is based on the belief that races are distinct' and went on to repeat the shibboleths of the American school.** Racism could be 'both intentional and unintentional' and 'a well intentioned and apparently sympathetic person, may, as a result of his education, experiences or environment, have negative, patronising or stereotyped views about ethnic minority groups which may subconsciously affect his attitude and behaviour towards members of those groups.' [41] And Rampton, like· Scarman, emphasised 'the particular educational needs' of particular ethnic groups – which doubtless helped the National Association of Schoolmasters and the Union of Women Teachers to pass off their 'negative, patronising or stereotyped' view of West Indian children for 'educational need': 'many West Indian children suffer from the fact they belong to a sub-culture of British culture with no readily identifiable distinctiveness' – in contrast, that is, to Asian children who are 'largely the products of a stable cultural background'. [42]

But Rampton also gave a fillip to RAT in schools. The Birmingham Education Department even got its 'multicultural outreach worker' David Ruddell, to devise its own teaching kit – on Katzian lines, of course, but adapted to British needs (as Katz had said one could do). So that although the basic 'philosophy' remained the same ('white racism is a white problem', 'racism = prejudice plus power' and all that stuff), the reality in British inner-city schools also demanded that some attention was paid to the racist violence of the National Front (NF) at whose instigation ('intentional or

---

By the very same token, however, a certain black radicalism has moved into the town halls and helped local organisations in the battle against the local state, as witness the Camden 'occupation' of the Town Hall in 1984 over the treatment of homeless families (many of whom are black), following the burning to death of a family in a sub-standard bed-and-breakfast joint.

**The report of the Swann Committee, the successor to Rampton, published as we go to press, emphasises attitudes and behaviour as Rampton does – but, unlike Rampton, does not see teacher racism as crucial to black underachievement.*

unintentional') innumerable black kids had been attacked and quite a few killed. But Ruddell gets over the difficulty with his opening salvo. 'One of the barriers to the recognition and tackling of racism today', he writes in his introduction to 'Recognising racism: a filmstrip, slide and cassette presentation for racism awareness training', [43] 'is the equating of racism with strong personal prejudice, with violence and the National Front. This is a vision of racism no less widespread among the teaching and caring professions than among the rest of the public. And it is a convenient and restrictive vision, for its allows the vast majority of racist thought and action to go unchecked.' Not all black people come face to face with 'this most extreme expression of racism', but 'all black people suffer the effects of subtle but endemic institutional racism that permeates our society and our culture'. And then, as though catching himself in the act of too brazenly writing off the experience of a whole class, Ruddell attempts to bring it back through culture – 'cultural racism comes as the luggage of our history, our language and probably our class structure' – but is baulked by the opposing culture of Scarmanite ethnicity and the cult of RAT. From there on, his pamphlet takes off into the higher reaches of psychologism to reach a screeching crescendo in Brenda Thompson's 'I am a white racist – but willing to learn'.

Another school of thought, emanating from the Inner London Education Authority, however, feel that there is an anti-racist element in multi-cultural education which they, as radicals, can exploit. Accordingly, they call themselves the Anti-Racist Strategies Team. But their 'Pilot Course' for teachers, for all its political posturing and anti-RAT rhetoric, has the same RAT outlook and even some of its training methods – such as 'Concentric Circles: an exercise to help participants to get to know each other', 'Simulation Game', 'Brainstorming and commitments to changing institutions and practices – a sharing of ideas' (and this under 'Strategies for Action' for Channel 4 (which, because it errs on the side of rhetoric, as opposed to analysis, has become meat for RAT courses). [44]

The Language Training Centres of industry, on the other hand, have gone over to psychological and affective techniques without necessarily espousing the Katz philosophy. They have, for instance, moved away 'from a narrow definition of language to one which encompasses all aspects of effective communication training and probes behind the actual words used to the attitudes beneath'. [45]

The churches fell for RAT much more easily and as of second nature: its credo, after all, was no different from theirs: you must change yourself before you can change the world. Racism, in RAT eyes besides, had the look of original sin. And there was a certain set ritual and ceremony about RAT exercises, even a RAT confessional and a RAT priesthood to facilitate your entry into a raceless heaven, and an aura of piety surrounding it all. But of course, the different church groups stress different aspects of RAT, as churches are wont to do. The Methodist Leadership Race Awareness Workshop (MELRAW), for instance, speaks of the need for 'becoming aware of the sin of racism and seeking forgiveness so that we can begin truly to work for reconciliation'. [46] On the other hand, the Ecumenical Unit for Racism Awareness Programmes (EURAP) sees 'Racism Awareness Workshops' as 'designed to help people to get free of the clutter of upbringing, of misinformation and prejudice in order to be equipped to tackle the abuse of power'. EURAP also stresses the need for periodical assessment 'to see whether effective practices have emerged'. [47] If tackling the abuse of power is the goal, the churches have the example of the World Council of Churches' material support (albeit short lived) of revolutionary movements in Africa. By comparison, they have had one-thousand nine-hundred and eighty-five years to assess whether or not changing minds changes society. But then, that is why RAT belongs in the church, but not, necessarily, the church in RAT.

Where RAT afforded immediate sanctuary to racism, however, was in the police force. The 1981 rebellions against the police and their state had discredited the police force on all counts and at every level. The Brixton 'disorders', in particular, had shown up the endemic and unrelenting racism of the force in its entirety. Scarman, in rescuing them and the state from such public and universal opprobrium, had let them off with a reprimand for 'racially prejudiced attitudes' (in the lower ranks) and a severe course of multiculturalism and attitude-training. Gratefully, the police accepted the sentence.

They had, immediately after the inner-city 'riots', made a stab at multicultural studies at the Hendon Police Training College – and even appointed a black lecturer, John Fernandes, to carry it off. But, after Scarman, the police were threshing around for a training programme that would change attitudes and behaviour rather than educate and inform. A Police Working Party was set up the following year, but even before it could report (February 1983), the Metropolitan Police Force, influenced by the work of the DRRI in Florida, went off into HAT, with all its attendant simulation games, 'experiential exercises' and role-playing. At the same time it entered into a joint study and experiment in RAT with the ILTC.

Multiculturalism, meanwhile, had died at Hendon: Fernandes' attempt to find an anti-racist strain in multi-culture had brought him up against the hard rock of police racism, both at the recruit level and the senior officers', and put paid both to Fernandes and multiculturalism. But RAT was waiting in the wings and, no sooner had Fernandes been suspended, found its way into the Police Training College – through RAPU, whose leading black light was also a member of the Police Working Party and Ethnic Adviser to Haringey all at once. The Fernandes case had, by then, blown up into an important political issue for blacks – leading to a campaign highlighting the racism not only of the police force but of the unions. [48] But RAPU and its black facilitators gave no thought or mind to dividing black struggle or placating the police with RAT placebos – reputedly for £600 a throw.* [50] But then, that is the type of commerce that RAT lends itself to.

RAT also abounds in the voluntary sector – among youth workers, community theatres, housing groups, advice centres, community workers, nursery managers, who because of the sense of vocation and commitment that have brought them to their jobs, are particularly susceptible to RAT potions.** [51] And lest their commitment should let the voluntary sector stray from their particular briefs, the Home Office has made it a point (through Voluntary Service Unit funding) to corral them into umbrella organisations in Leicestershire, West London and Manchester.

Then there is black RAT for black people as in RAPU and LRATU (Lewisham Racism Awareness Training Unit), for instance – concerned with recovering black identity and raising black consciousness and, in the stated case of the Lewisham Unit, with enhancing and strengthening 'practices that lead to power acquisition particularly within the confines of white dominated organisations and society in general'. [52] Inter-racial RAT (not advocated in Katz) has tended to dwindle of late, but still holds sway in bodies like URJIT (Unit of Racial Justice in Tooting), whose confused thinking and flagellatory rhetoric, as expressed in Tuku Mukherjee's *I'm not blaming you: an anti-racist analysis,* would border on the risible but for the seriousness with which they take themselves.

Finally, there are the professional RAT operators who appear to have come out of management training and business rather than from an involvement with black issues – and make a business of RAT. Foremost

---

* The police have gone into all sorts of RAT experiments since this, but a recent Home Office assessment on 'RAT for the police' has doubts whether RAT fits into the 'traditional culture of police training'. 'What the trainers were offering... were courses bearing upon the relationship between black people and white people. What the participants were expecting were courses dealing not just with the relationship between black people and the police. Clearly, the police did not want to be treated as whites suffering from racism but as police suffering from blacks. And RAT did not seem to be able to help them there, but a revised RAT, it was expected, has possibilities. [49]
The Home Office has, in any case, removed police RAT from private enterprise by setting up the Police Training Centre in Community and Race Relations at Brunel University (1983).
** I am grateful to the workers of the voluntary sector the discussions with whom at the GLC/IRR Seminars on Racism helped to inform my views.

among them is Linda King and Associates: Anti-Racist Consultants in Public Relations, Management and Staff Development. Founded by a black American woman, the firm has a leaning towards American concepts and American terminology such as 'internalised oppression', 'peoples of colour', 'parenting', etc. It even has courses for 'parenting in an anti-racist way' for mixed couples, that is. It also has cut-price courses, and gets written up in up-market (and sexist) journals like *Cosmopolitan*, where you might be surprised to come across words like 'slavery' and 'colonialism', but not after they have been treated to RAT. 'People can't help being racist', Linda King is quoted as saying. 'It is a form of conditioning which comes from our history of slavery and colonialism and present inequalities in the economic structure. But we can unlearn it.' And, of course, you must then 'choose to put into practice what you have learned'. [53]

The business propensities of RAT have also begun to be recognised in RAPU, the first and true church. Riven by schisms and sects and internal quarrels, its missionary zeal blunted by heresies and tainted by consorting with the police, and disappointed at seeing the money-changers arrive in their temple (when they themselves were being funded by the GLC), RAPU has fallen from grace.* But its (black) high priestess, taking note of the times, has set herself up as 'Affirmata', a 'Race and Sex Equality Training and Consultancy' in the manner of King. White racism, it appears, is no longer a white problem'** but a business proposition.

RAT fallacies and falsehoods

The confusion and fallacies of RAT thinking, as well as its metaphysics, have come through in the presentation. Thus racism is not, as RAT believes, a white problem, but a problem of an exploitative white power structure; power is not something white people are born into, but that which they derive from their position in a complex race/sex/class hierarchy; oppression does not equal exploitation; ideas do not equal ideology; the personal is not the political, but the political is personal;*** and personal liberation is not political liberation.

Some of the confusion arises from the wrong uses of terms. Racism, strictly speaking, should be used to refer to structures and institutions with power to discriminate. What individuals display is racialism, prejudiced

---

* *RAPU's anxieties are particularly noticeable at a seminar held at the CPP to assess RAT (31 October 1984).*
** *But if white racism is a white problem, why don't black people leave it to them to get on with it?*
*** *Changing society and changing oneself is a continuum of the same commitment else, neither gets changed.*

attitudes, which give them no intrinsic power over non-whites. That power is derived from racist laws, constitutional conventions, judicial precedents, institutional practices – all of which have the imprimatur of the state. In a capitalist state, that power is associated with the power of the capitalist class and racial oppression cannot be disassociated from class exploitation. And it is that symbiosis between race and class that marks the difference between the racial oppressions of the capitialist and pre-capitalist periods.

The fight against racism is, therefore, a fight against the state which sanctions and authorises it – even if by default – in the institutions and structures of society and in the behaviour of its public officals. My business is not to train the police officer out of his 'racism', but to have him punished for it – if, that is, he is meant to be accountable to the community he serves. Nor does changing the attitude of an immigration officer stop him from carrying out virginity tests – but changing immigration law (or merely the instructions from the Home Office) would. Nor can (middle-class) housing officers who have undergone RAT change housing conditions for the black working class, as long as the housing stock is limited. Nor, finally, does disabusing the minds of the owners and editors of the yellow press of their 'racism' prevent them from propagating their poisonous ideology of racism (when it sells papers); only a concerted continuing, public and political campaign can do that.

RAT, however, professes to change attitudes and behaviour, and thereby power relations – not in reality, but by sleight of definition: by defining personal relations as power relations.*

That is not to say that RAT does not act as a catharsis – for guilt-stricken whites – or as a catalyst, opening them out to their own possibilities and those of others, leading even to a change in their individual treatment of blacks. (The unit of oppresssion for RAT is the abstract individual.) It might even, for a rare few, open up a path to political activism, but such people will already have had such a potential, anyway and all that RAT could have done was to catalyse it. But its pretentiousness to do more is at once a delusion of grandeur and a betrayal of political black struggle against racism, and therefore , the state.

More importantly, in terms of strategy, the distinction between power and racism, – the distinction between power relationships between individuals (however derived) and the power relationships between classes (however mediated)** – helps to distinguish between the lesser fight (because

---

*Multiculturalism, on the other hand, denies power relations by denying the hierarchical structure of society.
**In Stuart Hall's brilliant and comprehensive phrase, 'race is the modality in which class is lived'. [54]

attitudes must be fought too) and the greater, and allows of different tactics for different fights, while clarifying at the same time, the different strands of another fight – so that the state does not play one against the other.

But then, the use of the term 'racism' both (personal) racialism and (structural) racism – influenced partly by the use of the term sexism, which itself arose from the tendency in the Women's Movement to personalise politics by personalising power (there is no 'sexualism' in the Women's Movement)* – has passed into common usage, itself a sign of the decline of the black struggle. And it would be pedantic not to accept it as such – till, that is, struggle again changes the terminology.

In the meantime, RAT has to be hoist with its own petard – it invites that metaphor to explain itself, mixed and confused. Racism, for RAT, is a combination of mental illness, original sin and biological determinism (which, perhaps, explains its middle-class appeal). It is 'the number one health problem in America', according to Katz – and if her disciples in Britain have not proclaimed it as clearly for this country (they have had no Mental Health Commission to back up such a view), they have, in their therapy, certainly treated racism on that basis.

Racism, according to RAT, has its roots in white culture, unaffected by material conditions or history, goes back to the beginning of time. Hence racism is part of the collective unconscious, the pre-natal scream, original sin. That is why, in the final analysis, whites can never be more than the 'anti-racist racists'. They are racist racists to begin with, born as they are to white privilege and power; but if they do nothing about it, 'collude' (consciously or unconsciously) in the institutional and cultural practices that perpetrate racism, then they are beyond redemption and remain racist racists. If on the hand, they 'take up arms' – or, in this case, RAT, against such privileges – 'and opposing, end them', in their own lives, at least, they could become 'anti-racist racists'. Racists, however, they remain in perpetuity. It is a circular argument bordering on the genetic, on biological determinism: racism, in sum, is culture and culture is white and white is racist. And the only way that RAT can break out of that circle is to acknowledge the material conditions that breed racism. But then it would not be RAT.

For that same reason, RAT eschews the most violent, virulent form of racism, the seed bed of fascism, that of the white working class which,

---

*The Women's Movement (in the West) personalised power – legitimately – to mean the immediate, direct and personal physical power of men over women, but then extrapolated it – illegitimately – to black and Third World struggle, which are connected more immediately and directly to economic exploitation and political power. [55]

contrary to RAT belief, is racist precisely because it is powerless, economically and politically, and violent because the only power it has is personal power. Quite clearly, it would be hopeless to try and change the attitudes and behaviour of the poorest and most deprived sectors of the population without first changing the material conditions of their existence. But, at that point in recognition, RAT averts its face and, pretending that such racism is extreme and exceptional, teaches teachers to avert their faces too. And that, in inner city schools, where racism affords the white child the only sport and release from its hopeless reality, is to educate it for fascism.* David Ruddell, Antoinette Satow and even blacks like Basil Manning and Ashok Ohri specifically deny the importance of the battles against the NF on the basis that such an extreme form of racism is not necessarily the common experience of most blacks and, in any case, lets off the whites with fighting overt racism out there and not covert racism in themselves, in their daily lives and in their institutions (meaning, really, places of work, leisure etc.). [56] But that is because they, like the activists of the Anti-Nazi League, but for different reasons, do not see the organic connection between racism and fascism. Martin Webster, the National Activities Organiser of the NF, saw it, though, when he declared that, 'the social base of the NF is made up of the desperate and the dispossessed among the white working class'. [57]

Nor does RAT, because it ignores all but the middle class, make a distinction between the different racisms of the different classes – the naked racism of the working class, the genteel racism of the middle class and the exploitative racism of the ruling class – if only to forge different strategies and alliances to combat the different racisms.

But then, to ask RAT to do anything so political is, as a Tamil saying has it, like trying to pluck hairs from an egg. RAT plays at politics, it is a fake, a phoney – a con trick that makes people think that by moving the pebbles they would start an avalanche, when all it does is to move pebbles, if that, so that the avalanche never comes.

And because, in Britain, black people have been involved in this con-trick – in introducing it, practising it, reproducing it – RAT has been able to mis–appropriate black politics and black history – and degrade black struggle. For if black struggle in Britain has meant anything, it has meant the return of politics to a working-class struggle that had lost its way into economism, the return of community to class,** the forging of black as a common colour of colonial and racist exploitation, and the opening out of anti-racist struggles to

---

*Ideas for RAT, as for the 'ideological classes', matter more than matter.
**It was that understanding of community and the resolve not to let it die that brought to the miners the unstinting support of Afro-Caribbean and Asian workers (See Chris Searle in this issue).

anti-fascism and anti-imperialism both at once.

Equally, if black and Third World feminism has meant anything, it has meant, on the one hand, a corrective to the personalisation of politics and the individualisation of power in the white Women's Movement and, on the other, an attempt to forge a unity of struggle between race, gender and class. RAT (which in Britain boasts black women in its ranks, some of them one-time activists) not only works in the opposite direction on both counts, but, in dividing the women on race lines reflects and reinforces the opposing feminist tendency to divide the 'race'on sex lines, and further disaggregates the struggle. Such fragmentation of struggle, while helping perhaps to overcome the personal paranoia that capital visits on different groups differentially, sends them off in search of their sectional identities, leaving capital itself unscathed.

Which is why even if there is no longer a classic working class to carry on a classic class struggle, the struggles of the new social forces must, for that very reason, focus on the destruction of the ruling class – for that there is, under whatever guise or name it appears before the respective movements: patriarchy, white racism, nuclearism or is conjured up by the 'new marxists': power blocs, hegemonies, dominant factions. And particularly now, when the technological revolution has given capital a new lease of life and allowed the ruling class to disperse and dissimulate its presence – in so many avatars – while centralising and concentrating its power over the rest of us.

References

1. A Sivanandan, 'From resistance to rebellion', in *A different hunger: writings on black resistance* (London, Pluto, 1982)

2. A Sivanandan, 'Race, class and the state', in *A different hunger*, op cit.

3. A Sivanandan, 'From resistance to rebellion', op cit.

4. See 'Race, class and the state', op cit.

5. Secretary of State for the Home Office, 'Racial discrimination' (London, HMSO, 1975) Cmnd. 6234

6. 'Race, class and the state', op cit

7. See, for example, Select Committee on Race Relations and Immigration, Session 1974-1975, *Report on the Organisation of Race Relations Administration,* 448-1 (London, HMSO, 1975), and David Smith, *The facts of racial disadvantage (London, PEP, 1976).*

8. *'Racial discrimination', op cit*

9. *See 'UK commentary: Grunwick (2)' in Race & Class* (Vol XIX, no 3, Winter 1978, pp 289-294).

10. 'From resistance to rebellion', op cit. See also Beverley Bryan, Stella Dadzie and Susanna Scafe, *The heart of the race:black women's lives in Britain* (London, Virago, 1986).

11. 'Editorial' *Race & Class* (Vol XXIII, nos. 2/3, Autumn 1981/Winter 1982).

12. House of Commons Home Affairs Committee Session 1980-81. *Racial disadvantage,* volume 1 report...,paras. 52 and 67 (London, HMSO, 1981), HC 424-1

13. K Young, 'Ethnic pluralism and the policy agenda in Britain' in N Glazer and K Young (eds), *Ethnic pluralism and public policy* London, Heinemann, 1983).

14. J S Bourne, 'Cheerleaders and ombudsmen: the sociology of race relations in Britain', in *Race & Class (Vol XXI, no 4, Spring 1980) pp 331-52.*

15. *J L Watson, 'Introduction: immigration, ethnicity and class in Britain,' in J L Watson (ed), Between two cultures: Migrants and minorities in Britain* (Oxford, Blackwell, 1977).

16. P Weinreich, 'Ethnicity and adolescent identity conflicts: a comparative study', in Verity Saifullah Khan (ed), *Minority families in Britain: support and stress* (London, Macmillan 1979).

17. Roger Ballard and Catherine Ballard, 'The Sikhs: the development of South Asian settlements in Britain', *Between two cultures,* op cit

18. Sandra Wallman, 'The scope of ethnicity', in Sandra Wallman (ed) *Ethnicity at work* (London, Macmillan, 1979).

19. The Brixton disorders, 10-12 April 1981: report of an inquiry by ...Lord Scarman' (London, HMSO, 1981).

20. Ibid

21. US Department of Labour. *The Negro family: the case for national action.* Compiled by D P Moynihan, (Washington, USGPO, 1965).

22. See also Martin Barker and Anne Beezer, 'The language of racism – an examination of Lord Scarman's report on the Brixton riots', in *International Socialism* (Winter 1982-3) pp108- 25

23. *Report of the National Advisory Commission on Civil Disorders,* Chairman Otto Kerner (New York, Bantam Books, 1968).

24. US Commission on Civil Rights, 'Racism in America and how to combat it' (Washington, USCCR, 1970).

25. P C Goldin, 'A model for race awareness training of teachers in integrated schools', in *Integrated Education* (no 43, January-February 1970), pp 62-64.

26. P Bidol and R C Weber, *Developing new perspectives on race: an innovative multimedia social studies curriculum in race relations for secondary level* (Detroit, Detroit New Speakers Bureau, 1970), and P Bidol, 'A rap on race – a mini lecture on racism awareness', in *Interracial Books for Children* (Vol 3, no 6, 1974), pp9-10.

27. R W Terry, *For whites only* (Detroit, William B Eerdmans, 1970)

28. Ibid

29. See Judy H Katz, *White awareness handbook for anti-racism training* (Norman, University of Oklahoma Press, 1978).

30. Quoted in Katz, ibid.

31. Quoted in ibid.

32. Quoted in ibid.

33. Ibid.

34. Nadine Peppard, 'Towards effective race relations training', in *New Community* (Vol 8, nos 1/2, Spring-Summer 1980) pp99-106.

35. Phil Baker and Elizabeth Hoadley-Maidment, 'The social phsychology of prejudice: an introduction' (Southall, National Centre for Industrial Language Training, 1980).

36. See Benedict Anderson, *Imagined communities: reflections on the origin and spread of nationalism* (London, Verso, 1983).

37. See the CRE report, *Local government and racial equality* (London, CRE, 1982); Joint Government/Local Authority Association Working Group, *Local authorities and racial disadvantage* (Department of the Environment, 1983); and the Conference which followed, 'Local authorities and racial Disadvantage', London, 21 March 1984 (Bichard Report): Race equality – strategies for London boroughs', report of the LBA/CRE/LACRC conference for councillors, Sussex 1-3 July 1983.

38. Home Office Press Release, 21 March 1984.

39. *Evening Standard* (16 October 1984).

40. Colin Brown, *Black and white in Britain: the third PSI survey* (London, Heinemann, 1984).

41. Committee of Inquiry into the Education of children from ethnic minority groups, 'West Indian children in our schools', Chairman Anthony Rampton (London, HMSO, June 1981).

42. NAS/UWT 'Multi-ethnic education', Birmingham NAS/UWT [1984].

43. D Ruddell and M Simpson, 'Recognising racism: a filmstrip, slide and cassette presentation for racism awareness training' (Birmingham, Education Department 1982).

44. 'Towards anti-racist strategies: a course for teachers' (ILEA Centre for Anti-Racist Education, 1984).

45. Nadine Peppard, 'Race relations training: the state of the art', in *New Community* (Vol II, nos 1/2, Autumn/Winter 1983) pp 150-59.

46. Quoted in T Holden, *People , churches and multi-racial projects* (London, Methodist Church, 1984).

47. Ecumenical Unit for Racism Awareness Programmes, Annual Report, 1983-4.

48. National Convention of Black Teachers, 'Police racism and union collusion – the John Fernandes case', (London, NCBT, 1983).

49. P Southgate, 'Racism awareness training for the police: report of a pilot study by the Home Office', (London, Home Office, 1984).

50. See 'Scabbing against Fernandes' in *Asian Times* (28 October 1983) and 'Racism Awareness Programme Unit', in *Asian Times* (25 November 1983).

51. For a description of a RAT course, and a critique, see the CARF articles in *Searchlight* (January and February 1985, nos 115 and 116).

52. Lewisham Racism Awareness Training Unit, Black awareness programme, 9-10 August 1984.

53. Denise Winn 'Would you pass the colour test?' in *Cosmopolitan* (January 1985).

54. Stuart Hall et al *Policing the crisis* (London Macmillan, 1978).

55. See Jenny Bourne, 'Towards an anti-racist feminism' (London, Institute of Race Relations , 1984) *Race & Class* pamphlet no 9.

56. See Ruddell, op cit; Ashok Ohri, Basil Manning and Paul Curnow (ed), *Community work and racism* (London Routledge and Kegan Paul, 1982).

57. Martin Webster, in *Spearhead* (May-June 1979).

GENERAL BIBLIOGRAPHY

CARF, R.A.T. – The Emperor's New Clothes, Searchlight, No.115 January 1985, pp. 18-19.
CARF, The Politics of R.A.T., Searchlight, No.116, February 1985 P.17

CHESLER, M.H. "Dilemmas and Designs in Race Education/Training", paper presented at Second National Symposium on Race Relations Education and Training, Washington, D.C. September 15-17, 1976.

CRE A Report on the Seminar on Racism Awareness Training held on 31 October 1984.

Davies, A. Racism Awareness Training – What's it all about? Voluntary Action, Vol II No.5, 14-16pp., June 1984.

Goldin, P.C. A Model for racial awareness training of teachers in integrated schools', in Integrated Education, pp. 62-4, No.43, January-February 1970.

Gurnah, A. The Politics of Racism Awareness Training in Critical Social Policy, No.II Winter 1984, pp.6-20.

Katz, J.H. White Awareness: Handbook of Anti-Racism Training, University of Oklahoma Press, 1978.

Nordlie, P.G. Analysis and Assessment of the Army Race Relations Equal Opportunity Training Programme: Summary Report of Conclusions and Recommendations. Human Sciences Research Inc., 1978

Nordlie, P. G. A Decade of Experience with Race Relations Equal Opportunity Education and Training in the Army: Human Sciences Research Inc; 1981

Ohri, A et al ed. Community Work and Racism, RKP, 1982.

Peppard, N., Towards effective race relations training, New Community, Vol XIII, Nos. 1/2 Spring/Summer 1980, pp. 99-106.

Peppard, N. Race Relations Training: The State of the Art, New Community, Vol. XI, No. 1/2 Autumn/Winter 1983, pp. 150-159.

Peppard, N., Race Relations Training: The Patrick Experiment, New Community, Vol. XI, No.3 Spring 1984, pp. 312-316.

Ruddell, D and Simpson, M. Recognising Racism: A Filmstrip, slide and cassette presentation for racism awareness training, Birmingham Education Department, 1984.

Ruddell, D. and Phillips-Bell, M. Race Relations Teaching Pack, AFFOR, 173 Lozells Road, Birmingham B19 1RN.

Shaw, J. Training Methods in Race Relations within Organisations: An analysis and assessment. New Community, Vol IX, No.3, 1981-82.

Southgate, P. Racism Awareness Training for the Police: report of a pilot study by the Home Office, Research and Planning Unit Paper 29, London, Home Office, 1984.